In the Women's Clubhouse

In the Women's Clubhouse

The Greatest Women Golfers
in Their Own Words

Edited by
TERRI LEONARD
Introduction by
MICHELLE MCGANN

Originally published by Contemporary Books, 2000.
This is the first paperback edition.

Cover image: Babe Didrikson, 1934. Copyright Getty Images

Cover design: Laura Shaw of Laura Shaw Designs, adapted by Joan Olson for the paperback edition.

Interior design: Joan Olson, joan@pagingjoan.com

Printed in the United States.

Credits appear on page 261–62 and constitute as a continuation of this copyright page.

ISBN-13: 978-0-9982126-8-5

Address inquiries to inthewomensclubhouse@aol.com

For Mike,
who introduced me to this great game.

Contents

Acknowledgments

To all the wonderful women golfers that are here in this book, I am forever grateful to you and the spirit of your words. Thank you.

I would also like to thank the former Ralph W. Miller Library in southern California, especially librarians Marge Dewey and Saundra Sheffer, for their help in my research. Be sure to check out "The Babe" golf course when you visit them. Special thanks also to Brian Lewis of Classics of Golf and to Peter Burford of Burford Books for allowing me to republish the Al Barkow interviews with Betsy Rawls and Patty Berg. To Betty Hicks, for inviting me into her home and sharing all her stories, scrapbooks, and pictures . . . plus I got to take her dogs for a walk! And to Barbara Romack, who cooked me dinner and told me some of funniest golf stories I ever heard. She also put me in touch with Mickey Wright, who didn't hesitate for a moment to allow me to reprint her articles for this publication. Same goes for Amy Alcott, Jane Blalock, Patty Sheehan, and Nancy Lopez. I am forever grateful for your generosity. I hope your words inspire the next generation of women golfers.

Thank you also to the late, great Rhonda Glenn. Her book *The Illustrated History of Women's Golf* was an invaluable reference in my research. It was an honor to know you, Rhonda.

A special thank you as well to the LPGA organization for its support.

My gratitude goes to my editor, Rob Taylor and publisher, John Nolan at NTC/Contemporary Publishing Group who recognized the timeliness and importance of this book during the LPGA's 50th celebration and to Laura Shaw of Laura Shaw Designs for the amazing cover. I'm thrilled now to be able to make it available almost seventeen years later.

Introduction

I fell in love with the game of golf when I was just a little girl. My father, who was a very good player himself, got me started at the age of eight. I was always a good athlete, but golf was a game I could play by myself. I didn't need a lot of other players, as in softball. My parents would drop me off in the morning at a par 3 course near my home on Singer Island, Florida, and I would play all day. Then they would pick me up in the late afternoon. I loved it.

Plus I was successful early on, primarily because my father put me under the supervision of a professional, Jean Noah, in West Palm Beach. She taught group lessons for girls on Saturday mornings. Fifteen or twenty of us would line up on the driving range and hit golf balls. Jean worked constantly on the fundamentals—the grip, the stance, and the takeaway. Even today, when I work with my pro, it's the same thing—the grip, the stance, the takeaway—the basic foundations of a good golf swing. Jean would tell us to go ahead and swing hard, not like a girl, and I attribute a lot of my power to her teaching. I have a long, fluid swing, and I've always had good fundamentals. In addition, I have always been aggressive with the club.

I also set goals for myself, even early on. I told myself I had to break fifty for nine holes before I could play in tournaments. Then when I had broken fifty, I had to break forty-five, or I had to break forty. There was always a challenge, no matter how well I had done. There was always something else to strive for. It is one of the things I love about golf—the fact that the possibilities for improvement are endless, whether you are just beginning to learn the game, or have been playing on the LPGA Tour for years. The only limitations are within yourself.

My father taught me to continue to work for perfection. Some people thought he put too much pressure on me, but during most of those early years on the LPGA he was always with me, carrying my bag in tournaments, making sure I was focused and working hard on my game. He gave me the support I needed. The only time he didn't accompany me was when he felt he should be devoting more time to my brother, J.C. My dad is a wonderful man. When I won the 1995 Takara World Invitational in Japan, he was on my bag, and it was such a special event—having him say, "We finally did it!" No one could say he held me back after that.

I finally did have success as a professional. In 1995 I won the Sara Lee Classic. On the final day I was paired with Laura Davies and Kelly Robbins, and even though I birdied the first hole to get off to a great start, the lead went back and forth all day. But I hung in there—it's one of the things I'm most proud of— even with the incredible amount of pressure we were under, and I was able to concentrate and maintain my composure and perform my best . . . and win. Afterwards, Kelly Robbins said I played so well, I deserved to win.

That spirit to go on despite the pressures is the reason I have so much respect and admiration for the women in this collection. They were, and are, all champions. Some of them I have played with, like Nancy Lopez, Amy Alcott, JoAnne Carner, and Patty Sheehan. Others, I have had the pleasure of knowing and learning from, like Judy Rankin, Kathy Whitworth, and Jane Blalock. And others, I have always heard stories about, like Glenna Collett, Patty Berg, and Babe Didrickson Zaharias. They are among the best golfers of all time, man or woman, and to hear them speak in their own voices is to understand the skill and dedication required to become the best. Some of them went through difficult periods, like Babe Zaharias, who won the U.S. Open a year after cancer surgery. Patty Berg came back after shattering one of her knees in a car accident, an accident that would have ended the careers of many players. And Virginia Van Wie, who was so sickly as a child that her parents taught her to play golf in order for her to get fresh air and exercise as a way of strengthening her body. She went on to win the United States Women's Amateur Championship three years in a row.

Some of the most charming stories in this book are the early accounts of women's golf. Mabel Stringer's reminiscences of golf in England at the turn of the century, where the women had a "wretched little tin tabernacle" for a clubhouse and were only allowed in the men's much larger and more substantial clubhouse once a year—using the back entrance—tells us how far we have actually come. And the stories of the early friendships that started on the golf courses and lasted through life make you realize that maybe things haven't changed so much at all.

The stories, however, all seem to present a similar picture. First, you learn how to play golf; second, you learn how to compete; and third, you learn how to win at the highest level. Many athletes have accomplished the first two, but have not learned how to do the third. That is the reason this book is so important, it contains the rare stories of the women who did accomplish this goal.

Michelle McGann, 1999

In the Women's Clubhouse

I

Ladies in the Rough

Beginnings

"In those days we had no clubhouse."
Mabel E. Stringer

Golfing Reminiscences

Mabel E. Stringer
from *Golfing Reminiscences*, 1924

Mabel Stringer was one of the pioneers of women's golf. Not only was she a first-class golfer, competing in the Ladies' British Open Amateur Championship in 1898, she was also a well-known golf journalist, calling herself "the first woman to write on golf as a profession." For five years she served as assistant secretary for the Ladies' Golf Union (LGU), the most influential organization in British women's golf, and she worked closely with Issette Pearson, the founder of the union. In 1924, she published Golfing Reminiscences, *a charming book recounting her career, her friendships, and her memories of the early days of golf when women were beginning to make the game their own.*

M y earliest recollections of the game date back some forty-five years or more, when as quite a child (a very wild child too!) I used to come across, in my bird-nesting expeditions on the Warren (now the Littlestone Links), a local parson and his two sons, all three arrayed in red flannel coats, trying to hit a small white ball with a "stick" among the sand hills. It appeared to me to be a particularly stupid, dull sort of game, far inferior to any of my enthralling pursuits—cricket, pole-jumping, bird-nesting, catapult-shooting, hunting, and the like. In due course, however, my education was "finished," and I speedily became a victim to the fascination of the game, and

the Littlestone Club having been formed in 1887, I might be
seen any afternoon, generally alone, knocking round the men's
links with a cleek, a heavy mashie, and my dear old trusty putter,
which I still possess and play with.

In 1891 the Littlestone Ladies' Club was formed, and for the
first five years of its existence I was its captain. Our links (fac-
tiously dubbed the "henrun") consisted of nine holes, right on
the shore. The first hole ran behind the Coastguard Station, and
the way from tee to green was infested with hens, and was the
playground of the Coastguard's numerous progeny: they made
sand-pies on the tees, they congregated in the bunkers guarding
the greens, and they picnicked all day *on* the greens; how, by a
merciful providence, they were not killed will forever remain a
mystery to me.

In those days we had no clubhouse, but were allowed the
use of two empty rooms in an unoccupied Coastguard cot-
tage, and knowing no better, we were hugely pleased with our
quarters. What the golfing girl of today would have said to
them it is not difficult to imagine! How well I remember the
pride we, the members of the club, took in our wretched little
tin tabernacle at Littlestone. How we slaved to get ready for a
championship. The men's club allowed only a meager sum for
furnishing, so we had to supplement from our own homes. It
was terribly cold and draughty in winter, for we only had a
rather more ornamental than useful oil stove, which in certain
winds refused to burn at all, or else emitted choking, smelly
black smoke. In summer it was so hot that we could not sit
inside.

Once a year, at Christmas, we had a mixed foursome competition, it being etiquette for the captains of the men's and wom-
en's clubs always to play together, and on this festive occasion
we were afterwards entertained to tea in the men's clubhouse,

but on the strict understanding that we were on no account to go in by the front entrance!

We enjoyed unrestricted use of the men's links; there was absolutely no rule to limit our playing whenever we pleased, and little marvel that we never went on our own course except to play our competitions, which were few and far between. We knew little or nothing about golf and golfers elsewhere. Littlestone was good enough for us, and indeed we showed our discrimination in so thinking, and persisted in our almost insular exclusiveness, until one fine morning in the early autumn of 1893 I received a letter from Mr. Wintle, the bachelor Hon. Secretary of the Littlestone Club, saying that a certain Miss Issette Pearson was coming down to see if the links would be suitable for the Ladies' Championship of 1894, and as he, being a bachelor, obviously could not entertain her, would I invite her, etc., etc. Now the name conveyed little or nothing to me, as during the preceding months I had been abroad in Eastern Europe, where the great news of the championship at St. Anne's, following immediately on the preliminaries for the formation of the Ladies' Golf Union (L.G.U.), had not penetrated. On the appointed day, Miss Pearson arrived. The next morning I played round with her on the men's links, and beat her quite respectably, not in the least understanding the somewhat uncomplimentary surprise at my having done so expressed by Mr. Laidlaw Purves, Mr. Arthur Adams, and other distinguished golfers who had accompanied Miss Pearson to Littlestone. Despite this misunderstanding, my friendship with Miss Pearson dates from the match we played on that glorious October morning over thirty years ago, and I am proud indeed to know that she is still my friend.

During the early days of the L.G.U., Miss Pearson and I were very much thrown together, and I found myself fairly launched in the golfing world. I went on the council in November 1893, and continued to represent Littlestone for upwards of twenty years.

As delegate in and from 1893 for the Littlestone Club, I naturally met all the prominent women in the golfing world. The first meeting I attended was held in the Freemasons' Tavern, in November 1893, and to this day I never pass the place without recalling my diffidence and shyness when I made my golfing debut in a public capacity. It was a very small gathering; as far as I can remember only the following were present: Mr. Laidlaw Purves, Mr. Arthur Adams, Mrs. Willock, Miss Pearson, and myself. Littlestone was elected as an affiliated club, bringing the total up to about twenty.

In the same month I went on a visit to Miss Pearson at Barnes, and she took me round to the clubs nearby. I played at Wimbledon, but I had a preference for the big, bad sand bunkers of my home links. During the months immediately preceding the 1894 championship at Littlestone, most of the intending competitors came down to practice, so I had the opportunity of meeting them all. Lord Eldon brought his two daughters, the Ladies Louisa and Margaret Scott. The latter was a fine golfer and a charming girl, aged nineteen at the time. She and I had a match, or what purported to be one, but she gave me the soundest beating I had hitherto had from a woman! I think I only won one hole when her ball was unplayable in a bunker. At that time she was in a class by herself in women's golf, and it is quite impossible now to compare the standard of play as set by Lady Margaret with the standard set in these latter years by Miss Cecil Leitch and Miss Joyce Wethered.

Thus and then began my connection with the L.G.U., which has continued from 1893 to the present day—an unforgettable period, full of incident, and brimming over with happy memories of people, places, and things.

Some Clubhouses, Then and Now

Let me just think back on some of the "shanties" which in the nineties were dignified by the name of "The Ladies' Clubhouse." First, there was my own home club shack which I described above, and which was by far the most primitive and uncomfortable of all. The next I was introduced to was that of the Wimbledon Ladies' on the Common, which at that time was really palatial (it had been one of the ranger's lodges), and where, moreover, in addition to a small lounge was a little tearoom, in which a real live paid attendant (Mrs. Frost) produced in an incredibly short space of time the most delicious little meals for lunch and tea from some invisible back region. Everyone had a red coat, for no one was allowed to play a shot on the Common unless garbed in scarlet. Play was only allowed on certain days—Tuesday, Thursday, and Saturday—but this restriction by the conservators only served to endow the club with some sort of extra exclusiveness and charm.

In the north things were very much the same. The St. Anne Club had a little corrugated iron building somewhat like ours at Littlestone, which was quite inadequate for the number of members but more comfortable.

So far as I can remember, the little shanty for the use of the lady members of the Hoylake Club was about the poorest of the lot; it did not even seem to stand straight on its own little particular sand hill. When we played the Hoylake Club in our tour of southern players in September 1895, we were entertained by the club to luncheon, but I cannot think that we all squeezed into this tiny, lop-sided shack. We may have done so, but I think not.

A great contrast was the splendid clubhouse of then West Lancashire Ladies' Club at Blundell Sands. This new clubhouse, with its twinkling windows and odd gables, is the prettiest of structures. And it is as charming within as without—a bright, airy sanctum, arrayed in lace curtains and striped sun blinds and dainty furnishings. In a word, a ladies' bungalow, in which one imagines many cool, quiet hours will be spent by tired players—if the noble pastime of golf could be supposed to tire its devotees. Every inch of space has been cleverly utilized: the corridors are lined with lockers; the hall and entertaining rooms are both lofty and commodious; and the kitchen is, as it should be, the best room in the house, and shining brilliantly with copper and brass.

There is one subject in which I unreservedly give way in favor of today, and that is in regard to the dress on the links. How on earth any one of us ever managed to hit a ball, or get along at all in the outrageous garments with which fashion decreed we were to cover ourselves, is one of the great unsolved mysteries of that of any age. I came across a description in an old book of the correct golfing dress in Scotland at the end of the eighteenth century (somewhere about the year 1775); but this, of course, only applied to men, and upon my soul I do not think it could have been nearly so uncomfortable as was our orthodox golfing kit thirty years ago, and was infinitely more picturesque.

The great wonder is that in spite of our clothes we actually did manage to acquire a certain proficiency in sports and games; and although it is obviously impossible ever to compare the relative merits of players of thirty or even twenty-five years ago with those of today, I believe Lady Margaret Scott, May Hezlet, and one or two others would hold their own with any of the ordinary international players of the present time. I can remem-

ber when the sleeves were so voluminous that we always had to
have an elastic strap round the left arm, or we should never have
seen the ball at all. It is within the memory of a good many of
the more modern players that "Miss Higgins" (named after the
American golfer) was indispensable on account of the width of
the skirts. "Miss Higgins" was also an elastic band, which was
slipped around the knees when the player was addressing her
ball, and was the most useful as well as the most unsightly of the
many inventions to counteract the vagaries and inconsistencies
of *la mode.*

When I first took seriously to golf the sailor hat was exclusively worn on the links. This was at St. Anne's. A few years later
the motor-cap came into fashion. It was quite smart in its way,
though was generally tied down by a voluminous veil which
was ugly and very stuffy to wear; but it certainly did keep the
cap firm on the head, and the hair did not blow down, or off, or
into one's eyes; for in those days no one "bobbed" or "shingled."

How on earth we bore the stiff collar is another mystery. I
can remember, and myself wore, all the grades of collar—first
the plain stand-up, then this was superseded by the double collar, highly glazed, and as deep as it was possible to wear it (we
used to literally peep over these), and sometimes one got a raw
sore all around the neck on the left side after playing golf in one
of these monstrosities. These in their turn gave place to the soft
silk collar, which, of course, has varied in shape since it came
into being. Then came the blissful no collar at all, which is, I
think, in summer the acme of comfort, but which, like everything else, has its drawbacks, in many blistered scarlet necks that
it causes. Then in the old days every self-respecting woman or
girl had to have a waist, and the more wasplike it was the more
one was admired. This was a terrible drawback at golf or tennis,
but for a time it had to be endured. The skirts had stiff peter-

sham belts, too, which were uncomfortable, and we sometimes wore two petticoats, which came down nearly to the bottom of the skirt and made it all very heavy and cumbrous.

The golfing girl of today should indeed be grateful that she need not play golf in a sailor hat, a high stiff collar, a voluminous skirt and petticoats, a motor-veil, or a wide skirt with leather binding. I repeat, she has much to be thankful for.

As one of the Ladies' Golf Union's first handicap managers, Mabel Stringer helped put the system we now have in place. However, the newly born system was in a chaotic state at the beginning because many of the clubs calculated the handicaps from a scratch score made by the best player in the club, ignoring the fact that if that player were matched against a true scratch player, she would need more than a few strokes to make the competition fair. Eventually, the system was reworked so that players of all ability could be competitive with one another.

My First Championship

Cecil Leitch
from *Golf,* 1922

When she was just seventeen, with a large bow in her hair, Charlotte Cecilia Pitcairn Leitch, entered her first championship with one of her five sisters. The year was 1908 and marked the beginning of her remarkable golf career. She had an extremely unusual but powerful swing that gave her tremendous distance off the tee, and along with the fact that she began to play golf near her home in Silloth, Scotland—where the wind, rain, and sleet were considered minor hazards compared with the heavy gorse and heather—it's little wonder she had won almost every championship honor in her time. Her first win was the French Ladies' Championship in 1912. She went on to win that title four more times (before and after World War I) and the Ladies' British Open Amateur Championship four times in 1914, 1920, 1921, and 1926. She also won the English and Canadian Ladies' championships. Here she recalls playing in her first championship at St. Andrews.

The year 1908 was a momentous one for me and my golf. From an obscure beginner I suddenly found myself a public golfer with a new-born reputation and a championship bronze medal in my pocket. It was like a dream, one of those delightful and romantic dreams from which one awakes to dull and unromantic fact. The transformation came so swiftly, in one short week. On May 15 I regarded myself as more or less a be-

ginner, a week later I was playing in the semi-final of the Ladies' Open Championship before thousands of spectators on the
most famous course in the world. Surely this was the stuff of
which dreams are made. And not only was this the first time I
had ever played at St. Andrews, but St. Andrews was, with the
exception of Silloth, the only 18-hole golf course I had ever
played on.

But to begin at the beginning and explain how it was that
my sister Edith and I came to enter for the championship of
1908. Friends and well-wishers had continually impressed upon
us that we played better than we knew, and that we ought to try
our luck at St. Andrews. Added to this constant pressure, our father was a Fifeshire man, St. Andrews appealed to our imagination, and our cousin, William Leitch Stuart, was a student at the
famous St. Andrews University at the time. Together these circumstances were too strong to resist, and we entered our names
for the championship, and eagerly awaited the result of the draw,
wondering whether we should come up against a Hezlet or a
Campbell or some other star who would extinguish our lesser
light at the first attempt.

When the draw did come out, a fortnight before the event,
it showed a record entry of 148, including all the big names in
ladies' golf, and it had treated my sister and myself with com-
mendable consideration. We were not at least to meet any of
the "champions" in our first match. We had both drawn byes in
the first round and curiously enough were to meet in the second two American sisters, Misses Marjorie and Marie Phelps, of
Brookline.

I was in the first quarter of the draw, my sister in the second.

Studying the draw, we were thrilled as we read the names of
those for whom we already had an enormous admiration—the
Misses Hezlet, Mrs. Cuthell (Miss Rhona Adair), Miss Doro-

thy Campbell, Miss Titterton, Miss Bertha Thompson. The draw had not been kind to Miss May Hezlet and her sister Florence, winner and runner-up the previous year at Newcastle, County Downe; it had brought them so close together that, bar accidents, they would meet in the third round. This they eventually did, with the invariable result, Miss May Hexlet, the leader, winning by several holes 4 and 3 to be exact.

In due course we arrived at St. Andrews and were instantly infected by the wonderful golfing atmosphere of the place. Our first practice round on the famous course was played with our cousin and friends who were then staying at St. Andrews.

We at once fell in love with the course, and have never fallen out of love with it. The spell that St. Andrews casts is lifelong.

I shall never forget my first match against a formidable lady opponent. This was Miss Heming Johnson, a Sussex county player, who, as she afterwards told me, was anxious to see how the "unknown flapper" played, and without any introduction came up to me and asked for a game. Needless to say I was delighted and gratified to be so honored. It was as pleasant as it was surprising to find myself able to hold my own in all departments of the game with such an experienced player. That was the beginning of a lasting friendship between Miss Heming Johnson and myself, and I never think of my first championship without a sense of gratitude to Miss Heming Johnson for her act of kindness in making a debutante feel at home. When we met in this first friendly practice round we had no premonition that we should meet in deadly earnest in a late stage of the championship. But that must be referred to in its proper order.

The international matches, which always precede the championship and sometimes take the bloom off a player's game, were the first excitement. I was, of course, merely a spectator, but my sister Edith, who had been "spotted" by Miss Issette

Pearson, always on the look-out for, and friendly to, youthful talent, was given a place on the English team, and "made good" by winning all her three matches. She played no. 8 on the team, her opponents being Miss Pim (Ireland), Mrs. Aubertin (Wales), and Miss Maitland (Scotland).

The next excitement following the quiet of a Scottish Sunday, was the stroke competition on the Monday. With a strong westerly wind blowing, it was not likely that scoring would rule low. Miss Elsie Grant Suttie, with 45 out and 44 home, was the only player to beat 90; she played the steadiest of golf. Two Irish players were second and third, Miss V. Tynte and Miss Florence Hezlet with 91 and 93. Though not especially bad under the difficult conditions, and at any rate better than the majority, my own effort of 100 could not be regarded as exactly auspicious. But that aspect of the championship was not troubling me, I was there to enjoy myself, to see and to learn, the extent of my hope being to survive one round.

Having drawn a bye I was not called upon to play until Tuesday afternoon, May 19. With nothing to lose and everything to gain I was in the happy state that knows nothing of nervousness, and I arrived on the first tee without a tremor. My opponent was Miss Marjorie Phelps and quite possibly she would have realized the seriousness of the occasion more if I had had my hair up and had looked less of a child. From the start things went well with me, so well indeed that I won nine of the first ten holes, the match ending 9 and 8 in my favor. Naturally the magnitude of my win excited comment and people began to take a little interest in the "Silloh flapper." Meanwhile my sister was being beaten by my opponent's sister rather heavily, to the tune of 5 and 4.

Two other sisters were debutantes at this championship, Misses E. and R. Grant Suttie, the latter being my opponent in the next round. Both she and her sister were pupils of little Ben Sayers, the famous North Berwick professional, whose wit and cunning have always been proverbial. I am sure I never expected to escape defeat at the hands of this player, but after a close match, which went all the way to the last green, I finished 2 up.

This brought me into the fourth round and up against Mrs. Harry Jackson, an Irish player from the Foxrock Club, and mother of Miss Janet Jackson, who has since won the Irish championship several times and made a big golfing name for herself. This round I won by 6 and 4.

I was not the only flapper in the meeting. Miss Elsie Kyle, a local player, the daughter of a doctor, about my own age, was greatly pleasing her friends, and at this stage had beaten Miss K. Stuart, Mrs. C. F. Richardson, and Miss J. Spence. Her play previous to the championship had earned her the reputation of a "dark horse."

By this time I was in company of the "last sixteen" and very astonished I was to find myself there, and to learn that my iron play and long run-up approaches were pleasing the critics. Curiously enough I had never been on a course where the long run-up shot could be played, and I just had to invent the shot that seemed best suited to St. Andrews. So quite literally this was an impromptu shot, the fruit of necessity, though quite naturally spectators supposed it to be a regular part of my game. I used for it a little light iron, the same club with which I played the half iron shot which was being admired.

My opponent in the fifth round was Miss Madge Sharp, a Scottish player from the Murrayfield Club and a hockey international. I remember we had a large following. One unusual incident made the match memorable. At an early hole Miss Sharp had the misfortune to play my ball and thereby forfeit the hole. There was a good deal of discussion about the incident, for some of the spectators, it appeared, knew that she was going to play the wrong ball, but refrained from telling her so in obedience to the strict letter of the law, though the spirit of the law would much better have been served had they managed to convey to her an adequate warning. Miss Sharp accepted the misfortune quite cheerfully and would not allow that it affected her play or in any way contributed to her defeat by 6 and 5.

I was now in the sixth round and one of the coveted "last eight." Miss E. Kyle was there too.

I shall never forget my next match, played on the Thursday afternoon. My opponent was Miss Heming Johnson, who had befriended me the previous week. An enormous crowd proceeded. It was ding-dong all the way, with never more than a hole between us; but I was certainly lucky to avoid one or two bunkers at the commencement of the round. An account of the match in the *Scotsman* said:

> "At the 16th hole Miss Johnson drove into the crowd on the left and her ball was interfered with, but she managed a half, the 17th however was lost. She drove into a bunker and had to play back, and she never made up the lost ground, while, to clinch matters, Miss Leitch holed out sensationally amid ringing cheers, with a run-up approach from 50 yards distance, and a 12-yard putt, where the cheering was renewed, enabled her to halve the last hole after a duffed second and to win the tie."

And so with fortune on my side I became the winner of a bronze medal at least. Miss Mather, another North of England competitor, whose championship debut had been made the year before, was also one of the semi-finalists. The most sensational match of this round was the tie between the local player, Miss

E. Kyle and Miss Titterton. For twenty-four holes these players, followed by an ever-growing crowd, battled before Miss Titterton could win. This constitutes a record tie for the Ladies' Championship to this day.

Two Scottish players fought out the remaining match, Miss D. Campbell and Mrs. F. W. Brown, the former winning at the last hole.

So Miss Titterton and I were to meet on the morrow morning, and Miss Campbell and Miss Mather.

That nerves were unknown to me is proved by the fact that I had two hours' sleep before dinner that Thursday evening, and twelve hours after!

It was a perfect morning when we set out, and my start was an auspicious one, for I was 4 up at the 7th. But at the 5th hole I found my brassie was broken and not being possessed of a duplicate, I began to fall back almost from that point.

Miss Titterton played a perfect tee-shot at the 11th or Eden hole, a one-shot hole of 148 yards, that finished 2 feet from the pin. The wind was dead against at this hole, and she showed sound judgment in taking a wooden club.

For the first time she took the lead at the 12th; I secured a hard half at the 13th (thirteen has always been my lucky number, for April 13 is the date of my birthday) by holing an 18-yard putt after Miss Titterton had put her third dead for a 4, I won the 14th, so we were all square with four to go. The next two holes Miss Titterton won in perfect 4's and she stood dormy 2. My backers looked very glum. They looked still glummer when I took 4 to reach the green of the famous road hole (456 yards) and was still some 12 yards from the hole.

Miss Titterton, however, was weak with her third, and 2 yards short with the like. To keep the match alive, I had to hole that long putt, and Miss Titterton had to miss her short one. Nothing seemed less probable. The first part, however, was achieved, for I holed my putt, to the delight of a large section of the huge crowd, whose cheering caused a young horse in a jaunting car to bolt across the course. Whether Miss Titterton heard the crash as the car was smashed to matchwood I know not, but she missed her putt, and on we went to the 18th, the home hole (360 yards). My drive was satisfactory, but Miss Titterton topped hers. The ball ricocheted along, hit the far bank of Swilcan Burn, rebounded thence on to the bridge, and finally came to rest on the fairway. Friends told me afterwards of their mingled feelings of hope and despair as that ball danced about as if it didn't know what to do with itself.

Miss Titterton made no mistake about the next, and we both reached the green in 3, and were down in 5 without any further thrills, Miss Titterton thus winning 1 up and passing into the final.

The other semi-final, between two dour fighters, required four extra holes before Miss Campbell could win, phenomenal putting marking the closing stages of this match.

The crowd that congregated for the final was worthy of St. Andrews, and so was the play that ensued. It was a great final in every way, grand fighting and grand golf, with a grand finish. Miss Titterton led by a hole at the turn. At about this stage of the match a terrific hailstorm burst over the course, but failed to damp the ardor of the spectators. However, the force of the storm brought down the R. and A. flag flying over the clubhouse, but left the L.G.U. flag bravely outfacing the elements, a circumstance which greatly delighted Mr. T. H. Miller, vice-president of the L.G.U. and one of its keenest supporters.

At the 13th hole Miss Campbell was 3 down. To be 3 down with 5 to go is a terrible position, enough to daunt anyone. But Miss Campbell was one of those whom nothing daunts, besides experience had taught her that a lead of that kind often has an enervating influence on the holder of it. So grimly and hopefully she stuck to her task, and actually won three of the next four holes, the two players standing on the 18th tee all square. A kind providence again watched over Miss Titterton's ball, for she topped her tee shot and, this time, jumped the burn. Had she not missed a short putt the match would have been over at the home green.

Away the players and spectators went again to the first tee. This hole, known as the Burn, is 365 yards, and short of the green is Swilcan Burn, a death trap for unwary second shots. Miss Campbell played short with her second, and Miss Titterton had to decide whether she would do the same or "go for it." It was a terribly anxious problem. On her decision might hang the issue of the championship. Her caddie, a typical St. Andrews one, put her brassie into her hand. Miss Titterton demurred, but the caddie insisted. "Well," said Miss Titterton, "I don't think I can do it, but if I do, I'll give you 5 pounds." The caddie was justified, Miss Titterton carried the burn and won the championship, and with it the admiration of all for a lion-hearted shot at the crisis of the match.

So ended my first championship, and I returned home with a bronze medal, so small in size, but so big in what it meant to me and my career. I was now really launched on my golfing career. I now knew that I could make a showing in good company, and I was just tingling with ambition and a determination to better my first attempt in the championship. One result of my play at St. Andrews was that I was burdened with the reputation of being a wonderful putter. When I holed that long putt on the 17th green, against Miss Titterton, a spectator was overheard to exclaim, "The child's inspired!" Well, putting has been called an inspiration, and certainly I did have wonderful luck with my putts at St. Andrews. But it is one thing to have a reputation, quite another, alas! to live up to it, and that early reputation has long since vanished into thin air.

Though some of the critics were kind enough to say I deserved to win at St. Andrews, I am glad I did not. It was the best thing for my golf that I did not go any further. Had I done so I might have rested content with my achievement. As it was, I set about developing my game, discovering the why and wherefore of everything, with a view to realizing what had now become my first ambition—the winning of the championship.

Golfing Incidents with Caddies

Cecil Leitch
from *Golf*, 1922

What self-deceivers golfers are! When they do a round far beyond anything they have ever done before they claim this as their true form. "I was in *something like* my best form today," airily said a 13-handicap who by a succession of inconceivable flukes had holed the course in a dozen strokes less than he had ever taken before. *"Something like,"* be it noted, intending his audience to realize that his golf was capable of still higher flights. Poor self-deceiver! He reverted to his normal 90's the next day and has never since been known to leave that decade save to soar about it into the 100's.

Alas! It is our average round that is our true form, and the performance that gives us our handicap. And if by virtue of a series of good "breaks" we get round in 6 strokes less than our previous best, let us not make too much of this feat. Far better to join the humble company of a certain golfer who, after playing rather worse than usual, said he had come to the conclusion that when he played well he was off his game.

There are those who condemn golf as a selfish game. They forget its philanthropic aspect. It gives healthy, harmless employment to myriad's of boys, men, and girls. And how these caddies add to the gaiety and human interest of the links! If one had time for studying them what an interesting study many of them

would prove. The old order has changed and caddies may not be
the sages they once were, but keen and intelligent caddies who
really identify themselves with their "masters'" fortunes are still
to be met with.

Personally I have generally been lucky in having good caddies,
and mention should be made of Wightman, whose valuable help
and advice at New Castle, Co. Down, were an important factor
in my winning the championship there in 1920. Throughout the
whole of my visit Wightman was only once guilty of an error
of judgment. He over clubbed me at a certain hole. Though this
error did not cost me a hole, my faithful henchman was much
upset and most apologetic. At Lytham and St. Annes in 1913 my
little caddie was equally keen and loyal, but I was a sad disappointment to him, and I can still see the big tears that filled his
eyes when I was beaten in the first round. My opponent in a
friendly match before the championship had a small mascot attached to her bag. Observing this and noticing that my bag had
no such symbol of good luck my caddie purchased one for me.
Although not bringing the desired luck, it is still in my collection, a treasured memento of a caddie's thoughtfulness.

The first time a girl ever "caddied" for me was in the French
Championship at Le Touquet in 1912. "Raimonde" was well
known to the visitors at that time, and I was fortunate to secure
her services. Her English was limited to a few words, but she
caused much amusement when she said, "a good, round, solid
British, *damn*," after my shot—we both thought well played—
buried itself in a bunker. What would her confusion have been
had she known that she was using a word forbidden to all except priests and parsons in the pulpit!

But not all caddies are so innocent and involuntary in their
lapses from virtue. Two ladies, accompanied by a very keen caddie, were playing on a very heavy course where the mud was of

a specially affectionate and clinging nature, so all-embracing in its affection indeed that after every shot the ball was more mud than ball. At one hole the keen caddie was sent forward to mark the balls where the ravine crossed the course. On the arrival of the players one ball found to be spotlessly clean poised on a worm cast, the other liberally plastered with mud and embedded in an atrocious lie. No word was said, but by an intentional slip or two the owner of the clean ball managed to halve the hole, to the evident disgust of her caddie, who looked the contempt he felt for one who refused to accept the good things the gods had offered.

In 1910 Cecil Leitch became famous for winning a golf match against former Men's British Open champion Harold Hilton and in the process gave assistance to the suffragette movement by proving that women could compete at what had, until then, been primarily a man's game. The media joked about the win saying, "Man twice Open and twice amateur champion defeated by a mere girl!"

Impressions of American Golf

Rhona K. Adair

from *Golf for Women*, 1902

Born in 1878, Rhona Adair was one of the finest players Ireland ever produced. She won the Ladies' British Open Amateur Championship twice, in 1900 and 1903, and the Irish Ladies' Close Amateur Championship four consecutive times from 1900 through 1903. Later, she was president of the Irish Ladies' Golf Union.

Known as a top competitor, Rhona Adair was a member of the famous Royal Portrush Golf Club in Ireland, and in the ladies' clubhouse there, you will find a display of photographs of Rhona with her trophies.

After a trip to America in 1903, she wrote the following article about her impressions of American golf. It provides a wonderful picture of how the relatively unsophisticated American women golfers were viewed by their more cultured and more experienced cousins in Europe.

I am afraid that this is a pretty big subject to write about, for, to tell the truth, my individual impressions are not quite so keen as they might have been had they not been fogged a bit by the wave of pleasure and all-round jollity into which I was plunged almost the moment I put foot on the steamship dock.

Perhaps the best starting point is by a compliment which I can pay with the utmost sincerity to the American woman golfer. It is one equally deserved by Mrs. Charles T. Stout (who is, I consider, decidedly the best American woman player I have seen), and by the poorest player that has been at any of the courses over which I have played.

This is in regard to their pluck. Never in all my experience have I seen such universal grit, sand, or what I believe you call "nerve" as is displayed by every woman golfer in America. It is really astounding. I don't believe that there is a bad sportswoman in America. Certainly, if there be one, I have not seen her. In England it is very uncommon to find a woman playing out a hole if she has been bunkered, or was driven out of bounds, or is for any reason what so ever playing several strokes more than her opponent. I find in America, that with the never-say-die spirit, which I have always heard was typical of all America, they keep right on playing until their opponent's ball is actually in the hole. Nor does this apply to one hole only of a match. I have seen women with a score of four down and five to go staring them in the face tee up with quite as much pluck and cheerfulness as they showed on the first tee, and in a good many instances with much more. That is the spirit which wins golf matches, and while I am loyal to the last to my home and friends, I must in fairness admit that American women seem better able to rise to a bad situation and play "better than they know how" when such a feat is demanded by the exigencies of the score, than either English, Irish, or Scottish women.

It may be that I have been particularly fortunate in friends whom I have made in America and in the atmosphere into which I have been drawn at the tournaments I have attended. But it seems to me that there is a much greater degree of good-fellowship and sociability connected with your meetings than there is on the other side. During a match in England it is quite unusual for opposing players to chat during the round as it seems to be unusual here for them not to do so, and in this way one, of course, they get much better acquainted than is possible when a round is made in silence, except for the formal courtesies and speeches of the game. Then, too, over here girls become better friends in a week's tournament than they would in England in two or three such meetings, and this, it seems to me, is one of the most charming features of American tournaments.

A point which seems most curious to me is the difference shown in dress when golfing by American women. At home we wear about the same things whether the weather is pleasant or unpleasant. Over here, it seems to me, the girls pay rather more attention to their clothes and general "get-up" when the sun is shining than we ever do. But they also go to the other extreme, and when the weather is unpleasant they simply do not care what they wear.

In England, dowdy and careless in dress as we are supposed to be, I have never seen women in such unbecoming and careless and rough costumes as I have seen here. So far as the nature of dress for play is concerned, I think we all dress about alike. A heavy pair of boots, any kind of a short skirt, and a waist which leaves one free for a good full swing are all that are necessary, and they are alike the world over. It is more common for women to wear gloves on the other side than it is here, I think, and that little detail is simply another link in the chain of pluckiness of which I spoke earlier, the inference being that the American woman would rather take the trouble to massage and manicure out the grime which she is bound to accumulate without gloves than to run the risk of spoiling a shot by a glove slipping in her grasp. So far as clubs are concerned, I don't see any appreciable difference in those made here and those made on the other side, although perhaps we at home use a slightly lighter club than the average woman here. After all, though, a good club's a good club, and must be suited to its owner and no one else.

Of the American courses I have nothing by praise. They far exceed what I had been let to expect, and while improvements could be suggested, one or two at which I have played rank quite on a par with the best links aboard.

Of course the nature of the soil is different, and so are the turf and putting-greens, but the latter average to run quite as true as ours at home, although they are not, as a general thing, so large. I think that the average of putting should be better here than in England, for the reason that your greens are much slower than ours, and the slower the green the harder one can hit the ball.

I have been simply astounded at the excellence of links which I have been told were only three or four years old, for we believe that a course must have been played over several years more than that number to reach its greatest perfection. Should some of the links I have seen improve in the next few years as much as they have in the past, they will be the best in the world.

American men may have an advantage over our masculine players through using a rubber-filled ball, but our women have adopted it almost altogether, and I think that its use not only improves one's game, but adds a deal of enjoyment to playing, as with it one is not compelled to exert anything like so much strength to achieve the same results.

This is a valuable point in any country, but particularly so in the United States, where I find that the climatic conditions are such that physique plays a very important part in one's golf. I think it is no exaggeration to say that it takes more strength to play an eighteen-hole round in the United States than to play thirty-six holes at home, and this is due solely to the atmospheric pressure and not to any appreciable difference in the lie of the land.

Despite this fact, however, I do not think that there is much difference in the length of carry one obtains from a shot, the ball flying to all practical purposes as well here as at home.

It is because of the fact that thirty-six holes of tournament play are too much to ask of woman in American in one day that I think that the qualifying round, as you play it here, is a decidedly necessary adjunct to tournaments. I thoroughly believe that match play is the truest golf, and hope that at home we shall always decide our tournaments by it exclusively; but with the big fields which you turn out here, one of three things must be done in the decision of tournaments. Either there must be two rounds of eighteen-hole matches each day; tournaments must last two weeks, or there must be a qualifying round, and this last is, by all odds, the best alternative.

There are, of course, other arguments in favor of the qualifying round aside from the one of time-saving.

In the first place, it teaches carefulness and steadiness, and steadiness is what the American player lacks more than any one other thing. Match play, with all its advantages, does induce a degree of carelessness in play when one feels that a hole is hopeless from the fact that one says, "Oh, well, one hole—what does it matter?" while in medal play, with every stroke counting, a moment's carelessness may mean loss of the medal or tournament.

One great fault, which it seems to me is very prevalent in America, is in the fact that American women devote too much time to perfecting themselves in one stroke, and not enough to the all-round development of their game. I found, in consequence, that the women here can average a much better drive than they can any other shot, for, as driving is the most pleasurable part of the game, they have developed their skill at that, without regard to iron-shots or putting.

American women really drive quite as well, if not better, than do English women, and, for this reason, I am convinced that the time is not far distant when the standard of skill will be as high on this side of the ocean as it is on the other. If a team of six or eight American women come abroad next year, as I hope they will, I expect our team to defeat them, but from what I have seen here we shall have to bring out our very best players and have them at the very top of their game to do so.

By all odds the best woman player in the United States whom I have seen is Mrs. Charles T. Stout. I consider her, all things taken in consideration, a wonder, while Miss Margaret Curtis is a phenomenal driver, and at times an extremely brilliant player. She is so erratic, however, that she cannot be considered as being in Mrs. Stout's class.

In fact, Mrs. Stout, I have been told, was considered by all good judges here to be quite in a class by herself, and from what I have seen I am quite prepared to accept their verdict as being true. Never have I seen a player display more ideal form than does she in every particular, and, in my opinion, she is quite the equal of any woman golfer in the world. Her play is a worthy model for every woman to pattern after, and, should she come abroad next year for the Ladies' English Championship, she would have a chance second to no one's of winning it. Besides the beautiful style in which she plays, the main beauty of her game is that it is so evenly developed, and not one stoke perfected at the expense of others.

Really, the only thing in which I found America much behind us at home was the caddies.

Much as I hate to seem unpleasant or captious, I must say that I consider the genus caddie, as found on American links, the worst fraud ever perpetrated. They know nothing; they are lazy and indifferent, and it is almost as much trouble to make them keep up with one on the journey round the links as it is to caddie for one's self. Generally they do not know one club from another.

At home the caddies are usually men who have been born and brought up on the links, and are really almost as much use to a player as a professional is here. They are uniformly faithful and courteous.

Rhonda Adair, who surprised many by beating the famous 'Old' Tom Morris at St. Andrews, was one of the first women to hit the ball hard and with gusto. She did not believe in swinging like other lady golfers; where "one persuades the ball on its way." She stood up to the ball "in a manner quite worthy of any of the sterner sex," as one reporter observed. "There is a determination and firmness in her address to the ball, which is most fascinating to watch."

American's First Women's Golf Course

Marion Hollins
from "Golf Illustrated," 1923

Marion Hollins's influence on women's golf in America is certainly re-
markable. Known as the "Golden Girl" for her athletic ability, Califor-
nia wealth, and famous friends, she won the U.S. Women's Amateur in
1921, the Metropolitan Golf Championship in 1913, 1919, and 1924,
and the Pebble Beach Championship a record eight times. With Alister
Mackenzie, she helped to design the Cypress Point Golf Club, a course
that many believe to be the most beautiful in the world, and with the
fortune she made by investing in the oil business, she again partnered
with Alister Mackenzie to design Pasatiempo in Santa Cruz, Califor-
nia—still one of the best courses available to the public.

She envisioned the need for a golf course built exclusively for
women, and in 1923 worked with golf architect Devereux Emmet to
design such a course in her hometown on Long Island. The essay that
follows describes this innovative venture and is the first writing by a
women on golf course design.

When I first satisfied myself that it was practical and time-
ly to build a golf course only for women the point up-
permost in mind, and one which I believe has been given due
consideration at every step, was to create a course that would

bring out the best in women's golf without sacrificing length or hazards. I felt that a course of this kind should not be of the usual standard type designed for men because it is impossible for most women players, despite the great advance made by their sex during the past few seasons, to cope with a man's course on equal terms with par or even with bogey. Only the long hitters had a chance of turning in anything like respectable scores and this has been a stumbling block for most title aspirants.

With this in mind the organization of the Women's National Golf and Tennis Club at Glen Head, Long Island, was commenced. Devereux Emmet was retained as architect, with Charles B. MacDonald and Seth Rayner assisting on the plans, and it is fully hoped that when it is all completed the course will develop into what is expected to be the last word, not only in women's golf, but in men's as well.

I went to England last spring to see what data I could secure as a framework for my ideal. Miss Cecil Leitch was of great assistance to me as were several other prominent professional and amateur players with whom I was fortunate enough to play a score or more of the courses. At Walton Heath I had the pleasure of playing both courses with James Braid. During the trip I made sketches and jotted down data which I turned over to Mr. Emmet for his consideration. Therefore one finds in the tentative plan several holes which are practically copies of famous holes on other courses while others have been laid out to embody the superlative feature of some of those which impressed me.

On my return I found the committee had progressed splendidly in the organization work. The piece of property selected is ideal in every way; the natural beauty of the terrain and the particularly fine topography combine to furnish the club with a background the equal of which few clubs have been privileged to secure. It was the best, in my opinion, that could have been chosen and its fine rolling qualities will undoubtedly appeal to the golfing eye. The club property is about one hundred and sixty acres but only about one hundred and thirty-five acres are being used for the course itself. A very choice area has been set aside for residential purposes and it is planned to develop an exclusive bungalow colony as soon as the course has been finished. Some of our friends who have visited the links have been so taken with this idea that they have already filed applications for sites. On the property is an old fashioned farmhouse, in splendid repair, which will be utilized as a women's clubhouse. This will be remodeled slightly to take care of the locker room and dining accommodations. The clubhouse is situated on a high knoll overlooking the course in every direction and from the first tee and finishing on the eighteenth green, all at the same time.

The response to our appeal for membership has been even better than our earliest hopes looked for. At the present time we have over three hundred members and all the money necessary to acquire the property has been pledged. Numbered in the list of subscribers are many women prominent socially and in the domain of golf and tennis. The vast majority of the subscribers are residents of the metropolitan area, but the club's roster includes the names of women from the principal cities in the country and one of the shareholders is a resident of Haiti and several from California. Practically every one, with whom I have talked, received the idea enthusiastically. Although our membership is more than three-quarters full we are receiving applications every day, but we have decided to keep the total down to four hundred, a figure we expect to reach within a short time.

To get a course on the lines I have outlined it was necessary to agree on a standardization which would permit a good average woman player to get home in two shots on most holes. I held a conference with several persons who were vitally inter-

ested and we all agreed that if an average carry for Miss Alexa
Stirling's shots could be arrived at, a good working basis as to
this distance would be arrived at. It turned out that Miss Stirling's drives, over a series of tests, averaged about 175-yards carry
and so this has been struck as the mean average in laying the
hazards in front of tees. By that I do not mean that all carries
on the direct line to the green are of that length. That would
be poor judgment. Mr. Emmet has just taken that yardage as
the point in the fairway where a ball would drop if the tee shot
was hit properly. Of course, in many instances generous leeway
has been made for the slightly shorter hitters or for shots which
were just a little off. Also on every hole there are one or more
alternate lines of play besides that of the direct line to the green.
This permits the shorter or cannier player to attempt a safer line
of direction, although usually it costs an extra stroke to do so.

The plan is only a tentative one. Several changes will be
made before work has advanced very far, but generally speaking
the plan will remain the same as presented. The clearing of the
woods is being proceeded with. Special attention is to be devoted to the ground in front of the greens, so that run-up shots will
always be possible. These will be kept in excellent condition—
in fact, just like the greens except that they will not be cut so
close. A special system of watering will be installed to take care
of the greens and fairways whenever necessary. Another feature
will be a separate fairway with a green at the end for practice,
constituting a regular drive and pitch hole.

The thirteenth is considered by Mr. Emmet to be the best
hole on the course, with bunkers projecting into the fairway
on the right and protecting the left flank also. This is a 210-yard
hole and some of the longer players may get home in one, although there is considerable risk staring one in the face at all
times. The alternate play for the short player calls for a carry of

150-yards, with a high pitch shot over the bunkers placed close to the green. The green drops away at the left and at the back, and there is little doubt that this is an exacting test of a one-shot hole for women. The par will be three, but it usually could be called a four.

The course has been so constructed that both starting and finishing holes commence at the clubhouse. The first hole proceeds in an easterly direction from the clubhouse but the ninth green brings the player back to the clubhouse. Starting at the tenth tee, which is also close to the clubhouse, the player invades another section of the course due south and then proceeds to work around until eventually the eighteenth green brings one back to the starting point. A particular feature, which undoubtedly will be attractive to most players, is that none of the holes are parallel and sufficient ground has been left between the holes so that a certain amount of isolation and privacy has been achieved. The course in itself is a masterpiece and promises to compare favorably with some of the best in the country.

While working with Alister Mackenzie on the Cypress Point Golf Club, Marion Hollins disagreed on the layout of the sixteenth hole. The hole, which is nestled against the scenic California coastline, was initially designed as a par four—a conservative dog-leg approach around the ocean coast.

Marion envisioned the hole as a challenging par three where the tee shot was directly over the water, the ball landing on the green 231 yards away, all carry. Being told that the drive was impossible, she teed up a ball right on the spot and hit it to the center of what is now the green of the famous sixteenth hole—a par three.

Lessons from My First Invasion

Alexa Stirling
from "The American Golfer," 1924

Alexa Sterling, who was brought up in Atlanta, Georgia, (in the same town and at the same time as Bobby Jones—even winning a childhood tournament against him) was affectionately dubbed "The Empress of Golf" to match Jones's Emperor nickname. With her impressive style and numerous wins she was a great favorite among the American galleries.

Her remarkable golfing career began when she won her first title at age twelve, and came to include three consecutive wins at the United States Women's Amateur Championship in 1916 and then again after the war in 1919 and 1920. Known for her calm, unperturbable style and her graceful swing, she was one of the first American women to focus on golf as more than just a recreation. She also won the Canadian Ladies' Championship twice, in 1920 and 1934.

In 1921, she sailed to England to try her hand at the Ladies' British Open Amateur and here records her adventures of that trip.

As it is approaching the third anniversary of the date upon which I sailed for England for my attempt to win the Ladies' British Open Amateur Championship, and also the Women's Open of France, a constant string of thoughts and recollections are parading before my memory, and it has occurred to me that perhaps some of them might be of interest to those who are patient enough to read this. It is true that anything I

39

may have to say may be more or less ancient history, but at the
same time, as I have never had the opportunity to describe all
the pleasant and amusing times I had, it may be as interesting
now as it would have been at the time.

As I had not been abroad for fourteen years previous to this
trip—I was quite young when I first went—I had naturally forgotten a great many of the customs and details as regards traveling. So I left all these details to my good friend, Josephine
Windle, who accompanied me on this trip and who returned a
year before after serving with the Red Cross in France. She was
the one who saw to it that when the Purser of the good ship
Carmania upon which we sailed was planning to give a dinner
in my honor that I was kept in entire ignorance of the prepara-
tions. So when we entered the dining saloon on that particular
evening, the whole affair was an absolute surprise to me. I felt
very much flattered that the knowledge of what I was attempt-
ing to do in a golfing way should create as much interest as it
evidently had, and that this interest should take the form it did.

The entire center of the Purser's table at which we sat was
covered with a miniature golf course, clubhouse, caddie house,
lake, and even on one tee a golf bag and clubs made of sugar.
Above the center of the table hung real golf clubs, and on the
menu, which was a special one, were the names of many familiar
places, all of which were supplied by the faithful and remarkable
Miss Windle. I forgot to mention that fortunately this dinner
was planned for the latter part of the voyage when it was more
or less certain that I would be able to be present. There was a
time during that voyage when even the sight of food would
have been so distasteful as to be obnoxious!

After landing on the other side and going through the ordeal of passing the customs, Miss Windle and I made our way
to the Adelphi Hotel which was our headquarters while in Liv-

erpool. On our arrival at Liverpool numerous letters from different people greeted us, but one particular note marked a red letter day in our trip for its results had a very decided effect upon our movements while I was in preparation for the championship which was to come off at the end of May. It was from Mrs. Temple Dobell, who, as Miss Gladys Ravenscroft, visited the United States and Canada in company with the then Miss Muriel Dodd. Between them they carried back across the water the championships of both these countries in 1913.

This note from Mrs. Dobell was of such a cheery and hospitable nature that we felt at home right away and knew that we were not to be allowed to be as two lost sheep—wandering about by ourselves. Mrs. Dobell herself was unable to meet us at the boat, but she asked her friend, Miss Doris Chambers, the present British champion, to come and see us at the hotel, which she did. We had a very delightful few minutes' conversation, during which arrangements were made for some golf at the small but truly delightful ladies' club just close to Miss Chambers' home,—the Wirral Ladies' Golf Club.

It was, I think, three days before I felt sufficiently up to the mark to attempt to play (the sea voyage had wrought havoc with my sense of balance) but I finally managed to get through one round. Even then I was not feeling very fit and do not remember many of the details except that it rained!

This was the very first round of golf which I had ever played in the British Isles. It was a memorable occasion for me and the course itself might bear a few remarks as it was the first of the courses especially constructed for women that I had seen.

The clubhouse was a small, unpretentious affair, but warm and cozy and surrounded on all four sides by the course, the eighteenth green being right at the clubhouse. In constructing this course, the limited space available must have caused some considerable worry for there was no more land to be purchased, all the surrounding country being thickly populated, and what land they actually had was all but too little. However, I think they did wonders.

After considering many other places, Liverpool seemed to offer as good opportunities for practice and play as any, so it was decided that as we had so many friends there, we would remain and I would prepare for the big event on the surrounding courses. We had splendid foursomes and twosomes with all those good folk who were so kind to us—and it was with great regret that we had finally to move north to Turnberry, for a few days' practice on the course where the championship was to be played.

To get from Liverpool to such an out-of-the-way place as Turnberry was at this particular time no small feat, for the great coal strike of 1921 was on and the railroads were consequently badly crippled with trains few and far between. Most of the trains, including the fast expresses, were discontinued from Liverpool to Glasgow, so we were forced to go another route which necessitated our making eight changes within a distance of approximately 350 miles. The few porters available were worked almost to death and so we were often without any help and had to do our own baggage moving. It was a great experience and one which made me realize what a fortunate person I was to have two good strong arms which I could put to work shifting baggage.

The trip was made in early April, and the weather on the west coast of Scotland at that time of year proved not to be all one might have wished. But even so, we had a very delightful time and I had an opportunity to gain much knowledge of the course and type of game necessary to play over it.

After a few days' practice we went back to Liverpool and then to London where more practice was put in and finally the date arrived to return to Turnberry for the championship itself. What fun it was seeing all the splendid players preparing for the big event, each one keen but very quiet and determined. A few days later, the girls from the United States arrived and this of course added tremendous interest and enjoyment to the gathering.

I can remember watching with keen interest from afar the methods of practice employed by Miss Cecil Leitch, for we had been drawn quite by accident to play in the first round of the championship and had known and realized for two weeks before the championship that it meant a short life but a merry one for one or the other of us. I had hopes, of course, that hers would be the short one and mine a trifle longer, but as it turned out, mine was the sudden demise, whereas Miss Leitch was to go through to be crowned again the Women's Open Golf champion of Great Britain with Miss Joyce Wethered as runner-up.

After this week of the championship, during which time I had learned to be a splendid spectator, we moved to London from where we went to France for the France championship in which I was a little more fortunate, being able to reach the semi-finals. That was as far as I could go, however, for again I died a sudden death at the hand of Miss Wethered.

A few remarks as to the differences between games of the American representatives and those of Great Britain, as I saw them, maybe interesting. First of all, the girls of the golfing world aboard are on an average much bigger and stronger than the girls of this country and I consider this a considerable asset. However, I do think that this superiority in strength is to a great extent offset by the constant wind and generally uncertain weather conditions prevalent in the British Isles. Therefore, it seems to me the discrepancy in strength and size between the girls of the two countries is pretty well evened up, as long as they stay in their respective countries.

In my opinion the actual style of play is much more graceful in the United States than abroad, on an average at least, but again it seems this ungraceful method of play is to a great extent due to the fact that the constant and tremendous winds which one is battling almost all the time, makes the players strike at the ball in an entirely different manner. The effort to keep a solid footing as well as balance and still keep the ball low does not allow of the fine body movement or swing which is almost always seen in this country.

The games themselves are not very different although the girls aboard do not use the high pitch with a quick stop nearly as much as we do on this side of the Atlantic. Here again is where the wind plays such an important part, for a high pitch cannot be controlled with a following wind and many times even a headwind makes trouble. I found this a thing hard to get used to when I was playing abroad, and I really believe that had I been more expert at the run-up shot, both for long as well as short distances, I could have taken Miss Leitch a hole or two further in our match.

If any who may read this contemplate going aboard to play golf, take a tip from me and devote much time and energy to the art of playing the low run-up approach, not only from say 70 yards or 80 yards, but even up to 100 or 125 yards.

Alexa Stirling was the first women player to break 80 in a golf tournament in 1925. She was quiet and yet extremely competitive, feeling that the serious player should never for a moment become complacent during a round but remain alert and focused until the last shot is played. She believed that the best golfers possessed nerve, courage in abundance, and the ability to concentrate under pressure.

Round Scotland

Joyce Wethered

from *Golfing Memories and Methods*, 1933

Unquestionably the finest women golfer of her time, Joyce Wethered pro-
duced an amateur record second only to Bobby Jones in women's or
men's golf. She won four Ladies' British Open Amateur champion-
ships and five English Ladies' Amateur championships before the age
of twenty-five. She was thought to be unbeatable, and generally was,
having lost only two matches in five years. And, like Jones, who wearied
of the strain caused by competitive golf, she retired in 1925, making one
final appearance at the Ladies' British Open Amateur in 1929, where
she defeated Glenna Collett in one of the greatest matches in women's
golf history.

Born in England, Joyce spent her summers across the road from
Royal Dornoch Golf Club in Scotland, and it was there that she
learned to play golf, developing a deep love of the game as it was played
on Scottish landscapes. Her writing is graceful, charming, and reminis-
cent of the finest writings on golf by anyone.

East Lothian

Everyone, including Doctor Johnson, must have recognized the
distinction between the road leading out of Scotland and the
one leading into it. No one appreciates the difference in emo-

tion when pursing these opposing routes more than I do. For the last ten years or so, I have been an inveterate visitor to this neighboring country; and although I cannot claim a drop of Scotch blood in my veins, I own to a feeling of absolute content whenever I cross the border. I have motored to and fro by as many as three separate ways, and that by Berwick, over the great bridge, is to my mind most like the correct gateway into a holiday land for the majority of English people. From Berwick it is only a short step to East Lothian, and the first stopping place for the golfer is generally North Berwick.

One reason, though not by any means the only reason, why I love Scotland, is perhaps the unworthy one that I feel I play better there than anywhere else. That is an inducement that no true golfer can resist. A course or an atmosphere that encourages one to play well, and flatters one's game, is a place to hurry to at all costs. It is not that Scotch courses are necessarily easier than our own. For one thing, they are usually less closely guarded round the greens, it is true, until perhaps an architect is called upon to alter them. This brings to my mind Muirfield. I played it once in the old days before it was altered and have played on it many times since. Sometimes it is said that penalty-bunkered courses are easier for low handicap players than what is termed the "strategic"; but I am not always quite convinced of the argument, though it has been well drummed into my ears at home by an eminent architect of our acquaintance whose chief happiness in life is to puzzle golfers and leave them in doubt as to the right shot to play. A "strategically" constructed course will probably produce these dilemmas for those to whom the experience of a course is still new; but once it is mastered, will it always continue to exert its misleading influence?

Whatever may be the truth of the matter, I have far too great a respect for the dangerous hazards at Muirfield to pretend that their only effect on the good player is to give away the correct length of the holes. Also on this particular links, when the greens are undulating and exceptionally fast, the slightest inaccuracy will land the ball in trouble only too readily; and when once the mistake is made a good recovery is very humbly to be prayed for.

However, I have never had to attempt to play the holes very seriously, by which I mean competitively; and Muirfield holds only the pleasantest of memories and matches for me. Nor can I forget the jolliest days of all, lying idly about on the hill tops, watching the amateurs and professionals fighting their way strenuously through the rounds of their championships.

Muirfield, North Berwick, and Gullane, are the three courses in the corner of East Lothian most familiar to me. In spite of lying so close to one another, each of them retains a certain individuality. Muirfield presents the serious, business-like aspect of the game. The matches played on it are usually four-ball matches amongst the men. As the headquarters of the Honorable Company of Edinburgh Golfers, and a course on which amateur and open championships are played, it stands in a high position in the golfing world and naturally takes its responsibilities seriously.

North Berwick, a few miles down the coast, has a totally different atmosphere. North Berwick, as I see it, possesses a dual character when it is in the season and when it is out. Sometimes it manages to combine both. Looking out on a bright sunny day over the sea to the islands raised high out of the water, like monstrous jewels in a low setting, and at the harbor situated to the right, a pile of picturesque, russet-red houses turning gray at the water's edge, is to be carried away by the beauty of the color, the vividness, and the striking reality of it all. The sparkle on the sea, the clearness and sharpness of the air, heightens the impression.

But suddenly out of this dream of beauty one is roused by a name shouted from the starter's box. The picture changes at once to a new North Berwick. Now the wild and primitive fishing town is transformed into a meeting place of countless friends and acquaintances—a scene of bright colored costumes, press photographers, and all the modern paraphernalia of a more sophisticated world.

I am not suggesting for a moment that it is not delightful to step into the midst of this light and spontaneous atmosphere for the space of a week or two. At the same time, there is an inevitable overshadowing of the genuine charm of North Berwick itself and its links; the feeling becomes almost too pronounced that the latest creations of Chenil and Fortnum and Mason are occupying the center of the stage. Even golf seems for the time being to be relegated to the background; it becomes merely a medium of sociability. Seldom is one alone, and never is a match concluded without a crowd of pleasantly chattering and distracting followers; for the links is a free and popular promenade for all who care to avail themselves of its attractions. No one would dream of visiting North Berwick in the season except to enjoy the life it offers. The invasion of visitors, however, ceases almost as suddenly as it appears, and North Berwick becomes its old original self once more. I have fortunately been able to visit it also in May, and then one can enjoy to one's heart content the prospect of this glorious coast line, running all the way past Archerfield. Alone by oneself on the links the scene is doubly impressive and lovable in its natural solitude.

Gullane, the last of the three, has not yet lost the quaint and rural character of the first tee. The way of approach is down the village street. One steps straight off it, as it were, on to a village green, to tee up beneath the shade of plane trees, their brown leaves dry and cracking underfoot. But seldom is one

allowed to linger. The sound of a buzzing bell and the sten-
torian voice of the starter summon the player to tee off and
leave this pleasant spot. The holes lead one straight (in fact, too
straight) up to the top of Gullane Hill, to unfold on every side
a view famous throughout the land for its wonder and distance.
Away up the Firth can be seen Arthur's Seat rising above the
smoke-laden haze of Leith; to the southward lie the Lammer-
moor Hills spread in a protecting belt which encloses a plain
of corn and barley fields; to the east and north the sea and the
Firth lie glimmering beneath us, dotted with ships and islands;
and over and across the water the slopes of Fife fade peacefully
into the distance.

I may be suspected of neglecting the golf too much for the
scenery. But how can one be indifferent where the beauty is
so distracting? I have found before now that, after playing on
a course, to come in and rave about the scenery is not always
taken as the highest compliment by those who are more famil-
iarized than we are by the surroundings and feel a special pride
in their home links. It suggests to supersensitive members of the
club that the links cannot have been fully appreciated. Though
this may sometimes be true (and I have known people fall back
on the merits of the "surroundings" when words of commen-
dation fail them as to the merits of the course), I do not think I
can ever be accused of offending in these instances. The links of
East Lothian speak for themselves, they need no advertisement
from members of the outside world. Everyone loves them and
every one revisits them.

St. Andrews

What a joy it is to jump into the train in the evening at a London
terminus, with one's club on the rack overhead, and to wake the

next morning to the sounds of Edinburgh and then the strange
hum of the train rumbling over the Forth Bridge. A few battle-
ships lie quiet and still far beneath, dull shapes in the hazy morning light which is slowly uncovering the stretches of the Firth
and the little groups of houses clustered along the shore.

It is a journey as full of charm and interest as the destination
we are bound for. The last mile or so runs down the side of
the links and the first exciting glimpse of St. Andrews is caught.
All too soon the train carries us ahead, wreathing the seventeenth tee in its smoke as it passes, then steadily on again by the
dreaded "station master's garden" (which, whatever it was once,
is now only a synonym for a goods-yard) into the gloom of the
station.

I cannot imagine a greater contrast to North Berwick than
St. Andrews. Its distinction lies in its being not so much a social
as a scholastic center. The University rises an impressive pile of
buildings in the very heart of the town. Students provide an
effective note of color in their bright scarlet gowns, whether in
the dark gray streets or mingling in a gallery on the links against
the dull green background. Nor are the more juvenile scholars
forgotten. They may be seen in scattered groups on Sundays, in-
vading the empty course and the sands on their afternoon walks.
On the very big occasions they sometimes join the golfing galleries, peering with apparent zeal through openings provided by
their elders. I can remember in the Ladies' Championship being
kept an embarrassed prisoner in the midst of a swarm of little
dark-blue figures from St. Leonards, flushed with the fever of
autograph hunting, and clutching stubbly pieces of pencil and
odd bits of paper.

The older inhabitants of St. Andrews may be indifferent and
superior to autographs, but all of them are golfers bound together
in one common enthusiasm for the game. It is talked of, thought

of, practiced by all. When I have stayed there, even in the shops I have found the same lively interest. The chemist hopes I am finding the course to my liking; the stationer asks me how I am playing; and the hairdresser to whom I have paid a hurried visit, is plainly more interested in my golf than in my coiffure.

It is useless to try to pretend that St. Andrews appeals to everyone. To some it may appear cold and unattractive, the links may seem a flat and dreary expanse, with too many blind holes, hidden bunkers, and bad lies. An unfortunate collection of faults to begin with, you might say!

To others St. Andrews appeals in all the glory of its past history, a battlefield that has been the scene of countless victories and a course requiring a never-ending stock of intricate and cunning shots to defeat the broken quality of the ground.

The first of my many visits was paid a number of years ago. I remember arriving in a state of considerable excitement as to what my first impressions would be. I had, of course, gathered certain ideas about the course, as only the year before my brother tied for the Open championship on it. I must admit that my first sight of the Valley of Sin, into which Roger's ball fell in his last round (costing him a five and the championship) caused me a sense of acute disappointment. It was pointed out to me from the window of the hotel—a small, uninspiring hollow, to be the cause of such an unhappy ending. I could not help inwardly hoping that Hell Bunker and the famous eleventh hole would come nearer to my grim expectations.

Driving from the first tee on the following morning, I was not altogether free from terror. My knees were inclined to be unsteady; the tee seemed a vast and empty space, and my ball and myself very small and insignificant in the middle of it. To make things more disturbing still, the large plate glass windows in the club overlooking the first tee was filled with faces. My

brother more than once that morning had called my attention
to the fountain to the right of the fairway, and I knew that the
object of his remarks was to inveigle me into hitting it, or at any
rate drifting in that direction. However, I saw plenty of room
away to the left and managed to pull a low drive into a region
of safety. The second shot happened to be a long one that day
and I barely carried the Swilcan Burn by a yard with a brassie. I
wondered whether it would be fate every morning to make this
perilous shot.

By the fourth hole I was completely befogged, lost and be-
wildered. On the last course I had played, the greens and the
bottom of the pin stared comfortably at me. Here I seemed fortunate if I could catch a glimpse of the top of the flag. Certainly
so far, except for the first hole, I had not yet seen any of the
greens to which I was approaching.

At this point, resigning all claims to independence, I en-
trusted myself completely to my caddie. For the rest of the
round I played obediently over bumps and bunkers, at spires
and hotels in the distance, and finally at the seventh hole—
with not spirit left to differ or to question—over the top of
a large shed which clearly belonged to a railway goods yard.
At the last hole, to my opponent's evident satisfaction, my ball
fell into the Valley of Sin, no doubt a fitting conclusion to a
bewildering round.

St. Andrews, I fancy, usually treats a visitor in this fashion.
At first sight it is almost impossible to grasp the idea of the
course. The good drives end in bunkers; the straight approaches
run away from the hole; the putts wander all over the greens.
To become a genuine lover of St. Andrews requires time and
experience. I stayed a fortnight on my first visit and the last
week passed in a flash—one heavenly day after another. It took
the whole of the first week to sort out the holes and begin to

understand the links, but ever since the Old Course has stood alone in my estimation, and I love every hummock of it.

The only way to discover what a course is actually like is to play it and find out for oneself. When I actually saw the famous holes, which have been so frequently written about, I found that they were quite different from what I had expected. I can safely say that the two holes that frightened me more than any others I have ever seen were the eleventh and seventeenth. There could scarcely be on any course two more alarming or more awe-inspiring holes. I have played them both at very critical moments, so I ought to know what a terrifying test they can be.

If I were asked which holes on the course I like the best, I should find it hard to say. They are all so varied and produce so many different reactions that it is difficult to pick out one from the other. Of the less famous holes, the second, perhaps surprisingly, has always intrigued me. The few bunkers in it are most uncomfortably placed and seem to lie in wait ready to gobble up a good drive or trap a too gentle or over-confident approach. To trickle slowly over the little ridge in front of the green is often the only way of staying near the hole; to attempt to pitch in the ordinary way is to leave the ball still some distance away.

Another favorite of mine is the thirteenth. A good drive may land one just to the right of the Coffin bunkers, under—but, it is to be hoped, not too near—the steep bank running across the fairway. Then comes a glorious spoon shot to be smacked right up to the large flat green, followed by a rush to the top of the rise to see if the ball is over the jaws of Lion's Month and yet has not faded away into the Hole O' Cross Bunker.

That is the great attraction of St. Andrews, that nowhere else is there a course so able to thrill, excite, depress, or frighten. You get the fullest value for your efforts. You can begin confidently enough at the first hole with the best intention in the world of keeping steady and returning (unless a tragedy occurs and who knows where that is not likely to happen?) some sort of a presentable card. By about the fifth and sixth other ideas may be creeping into your thoughts; the greens seem unaccountably large; the twenty and thirty-yard putts give the impression that three putts will be an inevitable certainty. But until the Loop is passed, hope never dies. If only a few threes can be collected, then the score is balanced for the time being.

After all, it is the long and magnificent homecoming that makes St. Andrews the wonderful test of golf that it is and gives the best player a chance of making up ground lost in the first half. The Long Hole In is famous the world over; the fifteenth, once the drive is safely steered from the tee, presents perhaps the easiest iron shot coming in. The sixteenth, distinguished by the Principal's Nose—a nest of three bunkers blocking the center of the fairway—drives the player, unless he is possessed of inordinate courage, away to the left, from which point the approach to the green requires a very perfect shot of its kind to finish anywhere near the hole.

The seventeenth threatens the successful scorer. The green can be approached gingerly, so that the Road may be safely counted out of the picture. But the bunker lying just to the left of the hole remains a danger up to the very last moment until the ball has finally been coaxed up the treacherous bank guarding the green. What a despairing turn the ball can take to the left just when the haven of the central plateau is thought to be reached! How many aggravating sixes can be recorded by being over-cautious! As for the last hole, it can scarcely be described as dangerous although it is certainly not as simple as it looks; the Valley of Sin has not earned its title in vain. Many times I have watched this hole being played in a championship week when a player, standing dormy and on the point of victory, is seen walking wearily to the nineteenth tee after failing to secure the necessary half.

The greatest triumph I have witnessed on this fateful green was in 1926, when Bobby Jones won the Open by six clear strokes from the rest of the field. His long putt for a three, I remember, just lipped the hole, and the crowd many thousands strong, could barely control its enthusiasm while he holed the little short one. Then they mobbed him, closing in with a rush and a burst of cheering which was almost frightening in its spontaneity. Looking down on the seething mass I saw Bobby hoisted shoulder high and carried round and round, the center of waving hats and outstretched hands. Such a welcome and ovation for the new champion, American by birth and in a land where the success of a Scot is usually the first and only consideration, spoke eloquently for the popularity of the winner. Later, in front of the clubhouse in his deep American drawl, he described what to him was the charm and character of St. Andrew's links, for which he holds an affection perhaps as great as that of any living person.

St. Andrews never changes. It is the same every time that one visits it. The holes remain unchanged; the same old characters greet one; the same long stream of townsfolk drive off the first tee when the day's work is finished. As they fade away into the distance over the Swilcan Burn we cannot but envy them their inherited possession.

North and West

In the north of Scotland golfing geography seems to repeat itself in rather a curious fashion. Just as Muirfield, Gullane, and North Berwick look across the water in the direction of St. Andrews within a circle of roughly thirty-five miles, so Nairn and Lossiemouth and Dornoch are contained within a similar area, with a belt of water between them, a few hundred miles further up the East Coast.

The golf is played in even grander surroundings; the land becomes more primitive and rugged. On the Moray coast, everyone would linger if they had the opportunity for a game at Lossiemouth and at Nairn, its less exposed neighbor, running along the shore among the stretches of purple heather. I have spent many a happy (and exceedingly cold) day on both.

But Dornoch, further away beyond Inverness, is my oldest and greatest friend of all the Scottish courses. In the first early stages, when golf seems perhaps more difficult than pleasurable, Dornoch taught me to grow fond of the game and showed me some of the delights it held in store. It would be difficult to imagine a greater incentive for the beginner than the low blue line of distance reaching beyond Dornoch Firth to Tarbot Ness, on the further side of which lies Cromarty and away inland the higher peaks frowning on the landscape. The first twelve holes of Dornoch are perhaps amongst the best twelve holes to be found anywhere. They follow the line of the coast towards the fishing village of Embo where the land seems equally good for as many links as might be desired.

It was here that I played in my first tournament. In the middle of August every year, the ladies struggle through a medal round and then qualify to play each other in match play during the two ensuing days. That is where I won my first gold medal. That knock-out tournament was chiefly memorable for the series of Miss Sutherlands, Mackays, Murrays, and Grants who came forward to offer battle. Visitors took part in these competitions, but the local celebrities formed the main bulk of the competitors—and very dour and accomplished opponents they proved to be on their native turf, whins, and sand dunes.

It was at Dornoch, too, that I first experienced the blissful sensation of breaking 70. An ambition to score a full-length course in 69 or under had been a secret longing for years past. I have since done it elsewhere, but the great day arrived when I played with Mr. Beaumont Pease who came with a party to lunch with us. I hope Mr. Pease will forgive me for boasting that I beat him 4 and 3 after he had gone round in 74. As he has had his revenge more than once, I feel sure he will be quite unmoved by this disclosure. Our best-ball for the first six holes was even threes and I know there was some lively giving and taking of odds on the result in the small gallery behind us while the match was in progress.

At any rate, I have for some long time loved a medal round. To rival or equal par never fails in it satisfaction. It must definitely mean that one has played well (and that is where the satisfaction lies) as there is no hope that this inflexible opponent will ever be off his game. The happiest three days of golf I have ever experienced were when I played six consecutive rounds— five on the New Course at Turnberry and one on the Old— and stood one over fours* at the end.

Mention of the West Coast brings me to Ayrshire, a county famous throughout the world for its courses. Just to the north of Ayr they run along the coast in an almost unbroken ribbon, the long and narrow strips of links even touching their neighbors at some points. Prestwick and Troon are the two outstanding courses and have been the scenes of the most crowded and congested championships that have taken place anywhere. So great is the interest taken in this part of Scotland, lying only a short distance below Glasgow, that the numbers who swarm to the great matches have become a serious problem.

---

* (The average score per hole for 18 holes is a 4 for a total of 72 strokes; so one over fours would equal a score of 73.)

The links at Turnberry are a glorious flat undulating space looking out to sea and to Ailsa Craig and the jagged peaks of Arran white with snow in the early spring. The new course at Turnberry is our favorite, amongst the deliciously scented golden patches of gorse. There could be no better place for the good-humored matches, amicable squabbling, and bickering over endless new styles and methods—whether for better or worse only time can show us.

Two Matches with Glenna

Joyce Wethered
from *Golfing Memories and Methods*, 1933

One of the most agreeable things about championship golf is the yearly alternation of the links on which it is played. If it were not for the "rota," which is a little of a mystery to me, and the variety of scene which the system encourages, a great deal of the charm of these meetings would be lost.

With me there were never any reservations as to which country I looked forward to most. Scotland has something about her golf finer and more characteristic than any other country, as is only fitting and natural for the land of its birth. I have the feeling, too, that the fiercest battles I have ever been engaged in which happened at Troon and St. Andrews could never have happened anywhere else. The air, the enthusiasm, and the play itself, seem sharper and keener in the north. Or is this only imagination?

It was my privilege to meet Glenna Collett in both these championships and my matches with her remain amongst the pleasantest of memories in championship golf. As an opponent she was unequaled in the generous-minded and sporting attitude that was natural to her. She has never been a player quick to protest against the misfortunes of a round. On the contrary, she has taken her defeats as well as her victories with a calm philosophy that nothing can move. There is no doubt that fortune has not treated her too kindly in her visits to this country; I believe there have been five up to now. Something has always just gone wrong on each of these occasions and an English golfer has seized the opportunity, when the moment arrived, to snatch a victory from her.

Of all the great players I have known, Glenna presents the most detached of attitudes in playing a match. She intrudes her presence to the smallest degree upon her opponents. I would even say that she appears to withdraw herself almost entirely from everything except the game, and her shots alone remind one of the brilliant adversary one is up against. If she is finding her true form then there is little hope, except by a miracle, of surviving—at any rate in an eighteen-hole match. But there are also some vague days in between, when her interest and concentration seem to be elsewhere. Her charm, however, to my mind as a golfer and a companion lies in a freedom of spirit which does not make her feel that success is everything in the world. Those who are so generous in defeat are the people most to be envied.

At Troon the match anticipated between her and myself was worked up to such a pitch beforehand that, when the day came, one of two things was almost bound to happen. Either we should rise to the occasion or one of us would fail under the strain of it. As events happily turned out for me, I played the best golf that I have ever succeeded in producing. With the exception of two poorish putts I know that I have never played the rest of the game so accurately or so well before or since. I have never strung so many good shots together (or so faultlessly for me) even if I have been able to produce similar figures (that is, fours for the match) by other and less correct means. But because I was hitting the ball so surely I was able to avoid what might easily have occurred under the stress of the moment—the slipping of one or two important shots and perhaps the loss of the match as well. I think this probably explains the reason why Glenna topped two drives at the sixth and ninth holes, strokes which as genuinely surprised herself, I remember, as they surprised everyone else. Unexpected as they were, they undoubtedly turned the tide in my favor, the second slip coming at a very crucial moment to make me one up after I had lost the lead at the short eighth by a weak putt. Up till that moment there had been nothing in it between us. Glenna had drawn first blood at the third, holing a very good putt for a three; I had drawn level at the fifth and taken the lead at the sixth only to lose it again, as I have mentioned, at the short "Postage Stamp."

On turning for home one up, I won the tenth owing to a loose third by Glenna, and the eleventh by holing a long putt. It was at this point that I again lived up to my curious reputation for not noticing trains. As was remarked in *The Times:* "Miss Wethered holed a long curly putt for a three characteristically enough with an engine snorting on the line behind her." But this time I was more fully aware of the reality of the train in question. It was puffing smoke in clouds behind the green in a way that could not very well be ignored. However, I was too well acquainted with the ways of a Scotch engine driver not to know that he was determined to wait to see the hole played to a finish before he continued with his goods to Ayr. Knowing this, there was little to be gained by my waiting. Besides, it was just possible that a train was not an unlucky portent. Whatever may be the truth of that supposition the putt made me three up and almost decided, I think, the result of the game. We halved the next two; at the fourteenth Glenna missed a short one and so gave me another hole; and a half at the fifteenth brought the game to a conclusion, 4 and 3.

The next time we met was four years later in 1929 at St. Andrews, and this was the championship that I certainly enjoyed the most. Perhaps one of the reasons was that I was able to enter after an interval with much less expected of me than usual. There could be no justification for such remarks as, "Of course you will do well," which in a game like golf spell ruin if they are believed for one moment. I was prepared for anything or everything to happen, however disastrous or extraordinary. It created an enchanting sense of freedom to feel that the well-meaning friends who come up after a bad shot and say, "That really wasn't like you!" would not this time allow themselves to be so easily shocked.

It has often been attributed to me that I entered for this event in a purely patriotic spirit, with the expressed intention of preventing any of the American invaders from winning our championship. I must really protest against this rather pretentious statement. The fact that Glenna Collett and I actually met in the final lent some color to the rumor, but I feel I should never be justified in entering for the sole purpose of hoping to prevent some other particular player from winning. A championship in my opinion is an event originally instituted solely for private enterprise and for the best player to win and it seems to me a pity that it need necessarily be converted into an international match on a larger scale.

At St. Andrews I did not, as a matter of fact, feel I need be weighed down by any responsibilities that might be thrust upon me. I was no longer a regular player in competitions. The moment had merely arrived when I could take part in an event to which I had looked forward for years.

The first round started perhaps somewhat appropriately in a very happy-go-lucky state of confusion. Phyllis Lobbett and I were timed to start between the awkward hours of one and two o'clock, and although a crowd had collected there was scarcely a flag-wager to be seen on the links. The first few holes were played with everyone running and rushing about in any direction he pleased. No one, not even the players and the caddies, knew where the balls lay. That they must be somewhere on the fairway amongst the feet of the crowd was all that was positively known, and this produced a bewildering state of affairs which made progress distinctly difficult. Eventually the arrival of more flags about the fourth hole helped to straighten out the mêlée, and soon after some of those whose luncheon hour had been disturbed drifted homewards.

In the next five rounds I played one Irish, one Scotch and three English ladies. Against Molly Gourlay I certainly played the best golf I had hitherto produced and was two under fours when the match finished.

In spite of a succession of good rounds, however, St. Andrews is not exactly a course where one can ever feel very safe. The greens are never sympathetic if one's putting is uncertain, and it is easy enough to lapse into a habit of taking three putts too frequently.

Glenna, I believe, was experiencing the same difficulty; she never struck the top of her form until the final round. I remember that she dined with us at Russack's on the Wednesday night, and I watched her as she walked over from the Grand Hotel, a charming and striking picture in blue and gold against the gray buildings. She was not particularly happy that evening, a little dispirited with the course, and rather depressed and dissatisfied with her golf; up till then only flashes of her true form had been visible in the matches she had played.

The next day she cheered up very considerably after appearing in something like her true colors against Mrs. Watson and Doris Park. She showed such convincing form in both these matches that I ruefully, and truthfully, prophesied that evening that there was trouble brewing for me on the morrow. To keep one's place successfully in a championship and yet reserve one's best game for the two or three last rounds is the most comforting mode of progress—much better than seeing one's game show signs of petering out the other way.

The final round was a match of the most extraordinary vicissitudes. Never had a close game swung in such a pendulum fashion. Glenna's first nine holes of the match, which she did in 34, was the finest sequence of holes I have ever seen a lady play. By the ninth green I was faced with a deficit of five holes. It was not that I had played badly through the green, but the putts would not go down and I frittered away my chances round the hole. If the touch of the putter leaves you at St. Andrews on those fast and immense greens, then heaven help you! You are indeed lost until you recover it.

I have always had the tendency to be nervous and rather jumpy round the hole in the early stages of a match and the only remedy that can cure me is to hole a good firm one. On the tenth green I did make a good putt of about three yards, but it just came out again, and that is no use from the remedial point of view! We halved the eleventh. The twelfth, to my mind, was the crux of the whole game. I believe that Glenna missed her chance there of making the match almost a certainty. We were both on the green in two and my first putt was woefully short. Finally, after I had missed the next, Glenna was left a putt of from three to four feet to win the hole. If she had become six up at this point of the game, due to my criminally taking three putts again, I do not think the result would ever have been a close one. But she let me off, missed her first putt of the match and left me a ray of hope.

There is almost always a quick reaction when an important chance is missed. Nothing can be so heartening to the player who is behind, and the mistake encourages a feeling of strain and uncertainty in the leader, however strongly he or she may be going at the time. On the next green I holed my first putt—a good one of four yards—and from that moment began to be able to get down the important ones. Glenna did not keep up her relentless attack and relaxed the pressure sufficiently to allow me to win back three of the five holes before luncheon.

Even then the position was none too good. My St. Andrews supporters had been through a black morning and the period during which I had been five down, I am afraid, had tried them almost as sorely as myself. A stranger, quite indifferent to golf, who was walking in the streets of St. Andrews bent on seeing the Cathedral and the University was surprised to find himself addressed by a postman in a depressed tone of voice as he passed gloomily on his rounds with the remark, "She's five doon." What the stranger thought of this unsolicited piece of information I cannot imagine.

The fluctuations and figures of the match continued to be amazing. Our best-ball score in the morning was 71. Glenna's deluge of par figures and under up to the twelfth hole consisted of nine fours, one three and a two. Then my turn of good luck began. From the 9th I took 73 for the next eighteen holes and in the afternoon actually stood four up at the ninth, a difference of nine holes from the position at the same point in the morning round. One might imagine from the psychology of the game that the excitement of the match was now probably over, and that all would perhaps end quietly on a green four or five holes from home. From any likelihood of such a peaceful ending I was rudely awakened by Glenna doing the next two holes in three apiece and winning them both. To lose two holes so abruptly altered the whole complexion of the game, and I must confess that I found the playing of the remaining holes a very trying experience. I had also the memory of throwing away a lead at Troon in a previous year which did not tend to make the position any more comforting. At the fifteenth the state of the match was still two up. I had in the meantime won another hole, but lost the Long Hole In, taking a number of strokes which still make me blush when I think of them.

The fifteenth finally decided the result. I had sliced my drive and was unable to reach the green in two. A poor run up left me still six yards from the hole with Glenna lying practically dead in three. It looked very like being only one up, and in such a crisis, with still three holes to go, anything might have happened. But the most opportune putt I have ever made came to my rescue. I holed the 6-yarder for a half and kept my lead of two, which I was able to hold on to till the seventeenth green. I did not feel in the least like holing the putt, and even when it was on its way I scarcely realized that it was going in. Generally there is an instinct about a putt which tells you what is probably going to happen. This time I had no such warning. I only remember feeling distinctly desperate and hitting the ball rather hard as the putt was uphill; and then the hole gobbled it up. Thank heavens there are still such happy surprises in the world!

The next hole we halved to make me dormy two. Then at the seventeenth, a very exacting hole in any circumstance, I was relieved of the responsibility of playing it really well, as Glenna took four to reach the plateau. All the same I shall not easily forget the anxiety of keeping the ball safely in play on nearing the dreaded green. It is the most trying of all experiences to keep cool just on the brink of winning; so easy to lose control and spoil it all. It was also impossible to ignore the pent-up excitement of the crowd which was ready to break out as soon as the last putt was struck. When the moment finally came it threatened very nearly to destroy us. Glenna and I were torn apart and became the center of a squeezing, swaying, and almost hysterical mob, shouting and cheering themselves hoarse.

Thrilling as was the wild enthusiasm around us I was gratefully relieved to find struggling at my side two stalwart officers of the law. After what seemed an eternity we were able to force our way, yard by yard, through the crowd to the road by the side of the green, and from there gradually to the steps of the hotel. How Glenna fared in the meantime I never quite discovered; evidently she escaped another route.

It was on being escorted once more on either side by my two friends, the policeman, to the clubhouse after the crowd had thinned a little, that I first realized the apparent ignominy of my position. Thoughts of stone passages, prison cells, and bread and water floated vaguely through my mind. It was only when the prize-giving and the speeches were over that I began to feel really free once more. Then came the awakening to the fact that the greatest ambition of my life had been realized after all—the winning of a championship at St. Andrews. As a finale of ten years from my first championship it seemed altogether too good to be true.

Joyce Wethered, who was known for her fierce concentration on the golf course, astounded the crowd at the English Ladies' Close Amateur Golf Championship in 1920 by making an eight-foot birdie putt on the seventeenth hole at Sheringham to defeat Cecil Leitch. Just before she hit the winning stroke, a train charged by on the railroad tracks adjoining the hole. When asked how she made such an important putt with such a great distraction, Joyce replied, "What train?"

The Making of a Golfer

Glenna Collett Vare

from *Ladies in the Rough*, 1928

Born in New Haven Connecticut in 1903, Glenna Collett Vare was truly a star of women's golf. She won the United States Women's Amateur Championship six times and several other prestigious tournaments. The Vare trophy, the LPGA award for low scoring average, is named for her. She was as important to women's golf as Bobby Jones was to men's. The women amateurs felt that they had a chance to win a tournament only when Glenna did not play.

Wonderfully competitive and possessing a long rhythmic swing, Glenna emerged quite suddenly on the amateur scene by beating the renowned English player Cecil Leitch in the Berthellyn Cup tournament at Huntington Valley Country Club in 1921. The only disappointment of her career was her failure to win the British Amateur where she reached the finals in 1929 and again in 1930.

Looking back over ten years of tournament play—at the ripe old age of twenty-five—and weighing forces which, blended together, determined my present position in the sport, it seems that nature conspired with chance and circumstances to fit me into the mold of a golfer.

There was little or no choice in the matter, like many others who are intensely interested in the sport, the love of competition and the outdoors was in my blood. My temperament, natural ability, environment, and inclination pointed to such a hobby and all I had to do was "follow through."

The long undulation of fairway, like a flowing river caressed by sun and wind, the white and regular splashes of bunkers, the sparkling emerald of the putting greens, with red flags fluttering astern over cups, unrolled for me much like a magic carpet over which I blithely walked to the heights.

As far back as I can remember, I was interested in some kind of sport; I could swim and dive at nine and drove an automobile at ten. My real interest, however, centered in baseball. I played with my brother Ned and his team on a field near our home in Providence, Rhode Island, until I was nearly fourteen; then mother suggested that I take up a game more becoming of a young girl. I tried tennis and would have continued to play the court game indefinitely if I had not accompanied my father out to the Metacomet Golf Club one afternoon.

Standing on the broad veranda, perched high on a Rhode Island hill, I watched Dad send a long, raking tee-shot through the air. The ball dropped far down the fairway.

Tremendously impressed, I hurried out on the course and asked for permission to play along with him. With beginner's luck my first shot off the tee went straight down the fairway. The length and accuracy of my initial drive stirred the enthusiasm of my father and several spectators.

"The coming champion!" shouted one sun-browned veteran, who asked me to duplicate my swing. His comments were followed by others of lavish praise and warm encouragement as I moved from hole to hole. I had a natural golf-swing. With the proper training and instruction, said my enthusiastic supporters, I could hit a golf ball as far as any of the women players, if not farther. Whether they were kidding or not didn't matter. Dad was elated and my head was bursting with the soaring dreams that only the very young and ambitious live and know. As I came off the course after the first game, my destiny was settled. I would become a golfer.

It was in retrospect as simple as that. No bypaths, no hesitation, no doubts. No longer would mother have to worry about my ball-playing with brother. No longer should I aspire for honors on the tennis court. The strings of my racket gathered dust, rotted, and snapped in protesting neglect. Golf was my game. My wagon was indeed fastened to a star—I dreamed of someday becoming the champion!

With such a goal in mind, I labored to find out the shortest route to the top. If there had been any flesh-and-blood biographies of leading golfers eminent in the sporting world a decade ago, one fourteen-year-old girl in Providence, Rhode Island, would have neglected her studies in the Lincoln School and found such a subject far more compelling in interest than the routine of the classroom.

The leading figures of the golf world stood out in my eyes with all the grandeur that the aspiring soldier or actress associates with a Napoleon or a Bernhardt. How did they reach the heights? How did the few leading golfers, not so different in everyday life from the featureless mass of players, come to excel? I studied and imitated and observed the actions of Alexa Stirling, Elaine Rosenthal, Marion Hollins, Mrs. Vanderbeck, and Mrs. Barlow in order to learn the mystery of their success on the links.

There was no mystery about it. There golfers excelled because they exercised faculties every athlete possesses in some degree or other. They were more accurate, more painstaking. They hit harder and had iron nerve under the strain of tournament play. They studied and improved their game. No mystery—but plenty of hard work and concentration.

As my father explained it, I might do the same thing, if I was started young, stuck to it, and was properly trained. Then, perhaps, I could compete with these leading players driving off the tee. Under proper instruction I could match ability with the great Alexa Stirling on the putting green.

With all the determination of one in whose heart the magic spark of ambition had been ignited, and bountifully aided by Lady Luck, the fairy godmother of the golfing Cinderellas, I started in—ten years ago—and have been hard at it ever since. Ten years bright with a wealth of friendships, the stir of competition, the heart aches and fierce joys that only a tournament player knows. Ten years with the sun-dappled fairway, bordered by trees and fields and lakes, my world, and I hope it will be for many years to come.

I just celebrated my twenty-fifth birthday, with many things to do before I put away my clubs. There is the British Ladies' championship, which I attempted to win three times and failed. More than once I have visualized myself, gray-haired and stooped, wearily trudging over the wind-swept fairways of an English course seeking that elusive title. In my ten years of tournament golf I've been lucky enough to win the United States national title twice, the north and south and the eastern three times, east coast and New England championships. I've also captured the French and Canadian Crowns, yet it seems that in this infernal irony of an existence some things, made desirable by remoteness rather than by intrinsic value, have a compelling glamour.

So I am still seeking that solitary crown. And next year, circumstance permitting, and the year after that if need be, I'll be taking the boat, or possibly an airplane, to the British Isles. Silly?

Perhaps, but what have we that fills so completely the niche of long-sought-after victory?

I do not want to forget, however, the stirring events that colored my first days on the links, especially in the years to come, when I am, with irritating frequency, ushered into the gallery by young girls marching to the heights.

It was my happy fortune to come on the athletic scene at a most significant time—a period when women were breaking through the barriers in all fields of endeavors, from politics to swimming the English Channel, or flying across the Atlantic. American women in the first quarter of the twentieth century have won two rights: the right of exercising the suffrage and the right of participating in sport. The second of these seems to be as important as the first for the happiness and welfare of women themselves and of the world at large.

In my own life so much has happened, with events tumbling down on one another, that, to put it frankly, it is almost impossible to recall with any degree of truth the days of my early life. Perhaps I'm still too young and too many things are happening just now to get a proper perspective of the years before I became imbued with the idea of hitting and chasing the little white ball.

I was born in New Haven, Connecticut, on June 20, 1903, but I remember little or nothing of that city because my family moved to Providence, Rhode Island, when I was six years old. We have lived there ever since. Even my school days in Providence and the time when I aspired to be a baseball player are now blurred and rather vague in memory, though cropping out whenever I meet old friends from school or the neighborhood.

Yet there was no golf tradition in the family. My father was known in his younger days as a bowler and champion bicyclist. I know very little about the bicycle craze that swept the country thirty years ago other than the fact that Dad won the national amateur championship in 1899. My penchant for going abroad seeking golf honors can be excused as a trait inherited from Dad, who toured Europe twice, meeting the best riders on the Continent.

But Dad is very fond of golf. When I showed an aptitude for the game, he taught me all he knew and then turned me over to John Anderson, a local professional, for instruction. My long hours of practice were sandwiched in between appearing in local tournaments. You can imagine me at the time; slim, shy, and very young, matching my game with matronly women, suffering fierce embarrassment when the interest of the gallery centered on my game. My position was all the more humiliating because I was regularly beaten after the first or second round of play.

Being young, impatient, and ambitious, I was terribly depressed at my slow progress. I was consistently long off the tee, but my work with the brassie and putter was pitifully weak, and I never seemed to have the well-balanced game that would carry me to the top. There was at Shenecossett Country Club at New London a professional who came to this country from Scotland and whose name was linked with the success of Jerome D. Travers, the only man in this country able to win the amateur title three times in the last twenty years—Alex Smith. Dad made plans for me to receive instruction from him twice a week. This practice continued for three years, both in the North and at Bellaire, in Florida.

Alex Smith not only was one of the pioneer Scottish professionals in this country, but is by all odds the most whimsical character. A great golfer, and a former national open champion, he applies to the game a vast native intelligence and has a natural impatience with lady-like hitters of the little ball, either masculine of feminine. He was, and is, a fatalist in golf. When the ball rolled against him—as the ball will do at times—instead of railing at the breaks or furiously setting himself to overcome his luck, he would just say: "Aweel, it's not my day!" He is also a quick man on the putting green. "Miss 'em quick" was his motto.

Alex gave me a happy philosophy as well as an improved way of handling the putter and mashie. He strengthened my driving to such an extent that when I was eighteen, standing five feet six inches and weighing a hundred and twenty-eight pounds, I drove a ball off the tee for a measured distance of three hundred and seven yards—thirty-six yards farther than the longest drive Babe Ruth had made at that time, and the longest drive ever made by a woman golfer.

My first round of eighteen holes was something of an ordeal. I don't remember a more unpleasant afternoon. Struggling along, missing more shots than I made, getting into all sorts of hazards, and finishing with the embarrassing score of 150, I was ready to give up the game.

The only thing that kept me interested was the thrill of hitting the ball far down the fairway—I did get off some fairly good drives. But what really renewed my interest in the game was the appearance of four youthful players at the Wannamoisett Club in Providence.

During the year of 1917, Alexa Stirling, now Mrs. Fraser, Elaine Rosenthal, now Mrs. "Spider" Reinhardt, of Chicago, Bobby Jones, and Perry Adair toured the country in a series of exhibition matches for the Red Cross. This quartet of youngsters played at my home course, and I recall the excitement that prevailed at the club over their splendid golf.

Miss Stirling had just won the national women's championship and she was reputed to be the greatest woman player in the land. Bobby Jones in that same season had made a name for himself by qualifying in the national amateur at Merion. He was just fifteen. Both Miss Rosenthal and Perry Adair had national reputations as youthful stars.

Naturally I was curious to see these famous players and awaited their arrival impatiently. My interest in the game soared when I saw how young they were—just one or two years older than I. I fluttered around the club in a high pitch of excitement.

Except for the players, I was the busiest girl on the links that day. Bobby Jones attracted the most attention among the men, with his head topped by a blazing red béret, he was a fiery figure, but I—and I guess most of the women—watched Alexa Stirling. The first thing about Alexa that attracted my admiration was her wonderful poise, especially under fire. She was never flustered, she never hurried. I believe that she possessed the perfect temperament for a golfer.

Miss Elaine Rosenthal was quite as impressive. She was not as contained or business-like as Alexa, but I remember the golf. She went around Wannamoisett course in 80, the last word in women's golf at that time, and the record still stands. I followed eagerly the footsteps of these two girls and studied every shot they made. I had never seen such golfers.

What happened to my own game after watching these golfers was a common thing for an aspiring player. When I again played, I was like one inspired. I did not think of my stance, of my hands and feet in connection with my swing. All I did was to endeavor to hit the ball, and I must say there was decided improvement.

The first big tournament I entered was the Rhode Island Women's championship in the fall of 1918. Up to that time I had devoted my efforts to improving my game, taking lessons with the club professional, and desperately trying to come close to the hundred mark.

My first appearance in a tournament of importance was anything by impressive. All the other players had gone out when I stood on the first tee, ready to drive off. I was as earnest and determined as though I was playing for the championship of the world. And I didn't even have a playing partner. Two women followed me and kept score, which was just as well, for I finished with a humiliating 132. The next day, when I looked in the newspaper, I had the dubious satisfaction of seeing my name at the bottom of the long list. My brother comforted me with the remark that "Well, anyway, you had more than most of them!"

However, I had my baptism of tournament play, and the next season, 1919, was a rather ambitious undertaking for a sixteen-year-old girl, starting in June and finishing in October, with ten formal tournaments listed. I managed to come through with rising success, although my debut in the first round of the Women's Eastern Championship at the Apawamis Club, near Rye, New York, almost ruined me as a tournament player.

Matched against a swift field, I was eager, nervous, and excited. Names such as Mrs. Gavin, Miss Hollins, Mrs. Jackson, and Mrs. Vanderbeck assured me that I was in fast company. The first day I was partnered with Mrs. Caleb Fox, the oldest player in the tournament. I was the youngest. We became the veritable target for a battery of cameramen, who followed us from hole to hole. It was just a few weeks before my sixteenth birthday, and I suffered from a severe case of tournament nerves. My brassie refused to cooperate, and my putter was as stubborn as ever. I came in with a 107. And that annoyed me. Although several of the topnotchers floundered terribly, there was little consolation for me simply because I had been playing my own course consistently around a hundred.

Then I suddenly realized that a hundred over the deserted Metacomet course with a professional by your side was a kind of golf not to be confused with the wear and tear of tournament play, with an army of boys with clicking black boxes hovering in the background.

Since that day, I must admit, my attitude towards crowds and championship play had altered. I've learned to steel myself against the little irritations and distractions encountered in tournaments. Yet I shall not forget the mood of disgust that followed my return to the club after my first round. I wanted to throw my clubs away, to forget all about golf and tournaments and crowds. This attitude was in turn followed by a feeling of impatience to get into another tournament and play the kind of golf I knew I was capable of. You see, I was infected with the golf disease that manifested itself in tournament matches—a fever that still persists and keeps me chasing the little white ball over the fairways year in and year out. My score for the Eastern was 214 for thirty-six holes. Mrs. Gavin, taking about thirty-five strokes less, won the tournament.

Then Alex Smith came to Providence and suggested that I take a few lessons before entering the National Women's championship at Shawnee-on-Delaware. Spurred on by confidence Alex inspired, I went around in 93, my best score to date. Alexa Stirling and Mrs. Gavin were tied for qualifying honors with 87. I finished eighth and felt pretty good about it. Then I was put out in the second round by Mrs. DuBois. I was not so discouraged. My little success kept the fires of ambition going.

I returned to school, late for the fall term, forgot about golf on the suggestion of my French teacher, who kindly remarked that she wouldn't mind my absences if I showed any proficiency at the game. I was not a remarkable French pupil either, and chances of passing the course went a glimmering when mother and I packed off for Pinehurst in the winter, entered the Women's North and South championship, was eliminated in the first round by Mrs. Ralph Hammer, now Mrs. Edward Stevens, then returned north and tried to go on with mastering my French. So far I was a dub at both things.

When I returned to Pinehurst in the early spring of 1920, it was next to impossible to do justice to my school work. My interest centered on the coming golf season, and whenever circumstances and weather permitted, I was out on the links. Up to this time I had not tasted the sweets of victory, but this did not lessen my interest in the game. In my mind, I suppose, was the hope of someday reaching a great goal beyond the rainbow. But for the present I was not concerned about it. I was having too much fun just playing the game.

My play improved under the tutelary care of Alex Smith. I concentrated on long drives and iron shots and was educated to a better understanding of the putter. The championship fever was not yet upon me and might have been delayed for some time if I hadn't won the Shennecossett Country Club championship. After tying Mrs. Barlow in the qualifying round with an 86, I pushed through to the finals. Matched against the nationally known Elaine Rosenthal, with never a thought of winning, I went out with everything to gain and nothing to lose, played my best game, and came home a winner by one up.

Victory was sweet indeed. The desire to win was very strong. Mother accompanied me to Cleveland for the National Women's championship, held at the Mayfield Country Club. Alexa Stirling was still supreme for the third time over a period of five years in this event. Encouraged by the laudable words of the sportswriters, I had a 93 in the qualifying round, the same as the year before, but instead of being eighth place, I was tied for eighteenth.

So even in a single year women's golf had shown a marked improvement. Marion Hollins erased a record that had stood for years and was four strokes lower than the lowest score that had ever won the medal. In the first round I met Miss Rosenthal for the second time that summer, and, by way of proving that my early victory had been but a flash in the pan, I was beaten this time 2 and 1. But in that tournament I was helped by watching the play of Mrs. Quentin Feitner, the formerly Miss Lillian Hyde, and Doreen Kavanaugh, now Mrs. Campbell from California. Mrs. Campbell had a graceful and orthodox style, after the manner of Miss Stirling and Mrs. Feitner, and later won the California state championship by defeating Miss Mary K. Browne. I was enjoying the tournaments more and more and could easily understand why so many people who did not play in the tournaments came to join the fun and get into the spirit of the game.

In the Berthellyn Cup matches at the Huntington Valley Country Club, in Philadelphia, I had the opportunity of matching my drives with those of Miss Cecil Leitch in the first round. My only hope when the match started was to halve as many holes as possible.

When I lost the first hole, I was almost beaten, but I rallied somehow to win the second hole and continued to hold my own until the end. It was a grab for glory and I snapped it up gladly. I suppose that Cecil was by no means on her game while I—well, I have had many an opponent play the way I did that day—was in a trance. I concentrated on halving every hole and had the satisfaction of figuring after each one that anyway I should be beaten much less than I expected. When the sixteenth hole was reached, I surprised myself by dropping a treacherous putt, and started the eighteenth, one up! I had a chance, a real chance, and tried to arrest the panic rout that so often unnerves me at this point. On the eighteenth green I only had to drop a ten-foot putt to win.

Taking my stance, measuring the lie, I gently tapped the blade against the ball. It moved slowly over the green. Like a creeping terror...

The acute agony of that second!

Straight and true to the mark, the ball flirted with the lip of the cup and dropped in, giving me the match.

Lady Luck certainly remained close to my side during this tournament!

To anyone else, perhaps the fact that I had beaten Cecil Leitch was unimportant—an off day for the champion! To me it was the beginning of similar successes. I had gained the much-needed confidence, my nerves were steadier, my shots bolder—no opponent held any terror for me now.

I continued through this tournament, winning the final from Mrs. William A. Galvin.

Although Glenna Collett was impatient when she first tried her hand at golf, her determination to succeed kept her impatience in check. She soon became the most respected and admired women amateur in the country. When she played in competition, she rarely talked with her opponents. Her concentration was so intense that she virtually withdrew from those around her in order to completely focus on the game at hand. She was not unfriendly with her playing partners, but she felt her golf demanded all her attention.

Competing with My Friends

Virginia Van Wie
from "The American Golfer," 1934

During the 1920s and 1930s, women's golf in America began to come of age. Among the best were Glenna Collett, Alexa Stirling, Marion Hollins, and Virginia Van Wie. Although only thirty-five years old when she retired from competitive golf, Virginia reached the finals of the United States Women's Amateur two times in 1928 and 1930, before actually winning the championship three years in a row from 1932 to 1934.

Because Virginia was rather sickly as a child, her parents introduced her to golf as a way of getting fresh air and exercise. In a relatively short time, she developed into a fine player and began to compete in local, then regional tournaments. Her greatest asset was her driving, which despite her slight build, was exceptionally long and accurate. She loved the camaraderie and friendships during her tournament years, and she was known for her modesty and sense of fair play.

During my stay in Florida last winter, I motored over to St. Augustine to watch the final round of the Florida East Coast championship, and who should I meet in the gallery but Harry Evens—formerly managing editor of *Life* and now editor of the *Family Circle Magazine*—who had been my partner in a two-ball foursome over that same course as a preliminary to the same event several years before.

Quite naturally, our conversation turned to the past tournaments—fading out of the old crowd and the entrance of the present field. Mrs. Hill and Miss Orcutt were the only two players entered in the Florida East Coast tournament who had also played there in the not so distant past. Mr. Evans had been present during the entire week of the 1934 tournament, and he wondered whether it was because he did not know the new players that his interest in the tournament had lessened, or whether it was that the attitude of the players had changed. The golf was a good. The scores proved that in spite of adverse weather conditions. He asked me if I had noticed any difference in competitive golf, and when I admitted I had, he asked me why I had not written an article on the subject. It is a difficult subject to broach, and it is hard to express oneself clearly on it without some possible misunderstanding. However, for the sake of those starting to play competitive golf, I am going to try to define this difference.

There are many capable young golfers coming into prominence now—all striving to reach the heights—grasping for every bit of information that will hasten their rise to the top. I know this, because I was once in the same position. Now that I have arrived at my destination, there is only one bit of information which I feel is truly important. Consequently, I am writing this in the hope that it may help some of them. Outlining parts of my own experiences I believe may be the best way to express what I mean.

The girls Mr. Evans knew when he was so interested in that tournament were the girls I met in competition when I started tournament golf. The same group met in practically all of the Southern tournaments and became good friends. We played for several weeks in succession—a different tournament each week—exchanging honors for first place quite often unless

Glenna Collett played, when we were almost always forced to a lower position, for she undoubtedly surpassed us in ability, which none of us objected to recognizing. Her sportsmanship was as great as her mastery of golf shots.

My turn to be fodder for Glenna's ability came rather abruptly. It was my first meeting with her, and a great fear arose within me. The same fear haunts any new competitive golfer— that of having to match your shots against someone with greater ones. You fear you cannot do your best, which you are positive you won't be good enough anyway, unless she is having an off-day. Under a strain of this sort, I went to the course that afternoon and discovered it was possible to play very well with such a turmoil within me.

I won that match on the nineteenth hole. Naturally, I shall never forget it, but, what is more important, I shall not forget the consideration shown me by Glenna that day. She knew how nervous I was, but rather than take advantage of it, she honestly made an effort to get me over it. She is the type of golfer who prefers to match shots with you rather than see you mentally upset to the extent that you are incapable of playing good golf shots.

The majority of our group had the same attitude toward competition. It was your ability against theirs that mattered. The fact that we were all good friends and that many of the titles we were playing for were not too important undoubtedly had a great deal to do with this attitude, but it made competitive golf delightful. I played well that first year and had my share of victories in the more serious tournaments. Then came the inevitable slump which almost every beginner experiences.

During that period, I met one defeat after another. This was unpleasant and at times discouraging. However, the art of losing is a fine thing to learn. It is during such a period that well-meaning acquaintances offer so much advice. Due perhaps to my good fortune in winning quite a few matches earlier that year, my ability to execute golf shots was not questioned. It had to be my attitude that was wrong. I had to fight. My opponents felt too comfortable playing against me. I made it too easy for them.

I tried to acquire the "fight attitude." Someone had once told me I would have to decide whether I wanted to be a great golfer or a sweet kid before I could ever win a big title. This seemed an odd decision to be called upon to make. Fortunately, I eventually found it unnecessary. I did want to become a great golfer, but the disposition I had been born with could not be made over. Concentration does not come easy to me, and I was apt to talk to friends in the gallery too much, thus losing a certain amount of concentration in thinking out and playing my next shot. My attitude toward the people around me during a match had to be changed. I now do my conversing after the match is over.

Fight! Fight! Fight! That "I'll get you" feeling toward an opponent is something I have never found necessary, and when I feel it is, golf will cease to be a pleasure. Why is that feeling always preached to a young golfer? After all, if you hold the majority of the good cards, you stand a fine chance of beating Culbertson at bridge. My theory is this: If you perfect your golf shots, your opponent will need more than an unfriendly attitude to defeat you.

One's fighting ability is generally judged by the number of difficult matches one wins. Yet the first time I heard myself being judged a poor fighter came after a week of winning four of the hardest matches I ever played. I lost the fifth by a margin of 13 and 12, and that match apparently erased the merits of the other four. To be a good fighter means but one thing in my estimation: never stop trying to hit your shots perfectly. The good breaks won't always come your way—make the most of them when they do—and when they don't, keep trying to do your best. Should you lose, chalk it up to experience and take your defeat graciously. The good breaks will come your way another day.

It irritates me no end to hear a good golfer who has lost a match called a "poor match player," which is just another form of saying "poor fighter." That player eventually hears the remark and promptly adopts the attitude of "I will show you I can fight" and in the next match starts out with the sole intention of downing his or her opponent any way possible. With this aggressive attitude prevailing, the game turns into a battle of personalities and golf is placed in the background.

It is my belief that this attitude of aggressiveness is far more prevalent in competitive golf today than it used to be. It creates poor sportsmanship and spoils the joy of the game for the players and the pleasure of watching a shot-matching game for the gallery.

This is not true of all matches, but more of them are played in such a manner today than was true a few years ago. The reason for this, I believe, is the constant preaching of Fight, Fight, Fight, and the lack of understanding what the word means when used in connection with a golf match. Since I started tournament golf, no one has won so consistently as Glenna Collett Vare, yet I have never seen Glenna anything but friendly and considerate in a golf match. If you can play better golf shots, the match is yours. If not, it's just too bad for you.

Last year Helen Hicks and I faced each other in the final round of thirty-six holes for the national championship. We had been teammates in the International Matches held in England in 1932, and we had been training together for this championship for several weeks. In fact, we were both house guests of Ralph Bards in Highland Park, Illinois, during the tournament.

We had breakfast together the morning of the final, drove to the course in the same car, and, though the match was equally important to each of us, there was no feeling of enmity. Helen played the better golf during the morning round, and I was two holes behind when it ended. The afternoon round started, and I happened to have a streak of the best golf I have ever played in my life. On the last nine holes we played, Helen took 36 strokes and I took 32. The match ended in a 4 and 3 victory for me. The entire match had been a battle of golf shots—a pleasure to play and, unless a great many people were being untruthful, a pleasure to watch.

Swinging the Clubhead

Virginia Van Wie
from "The American Golfer," 1934

G olf is so simple it is difficult. That may be a strange statement, but I believe a true one. When Mr. Ernest Jones tied
a jack knife to a corner of a large handkerchief and proved to
me what swinging actually meant and what a real swing felt like,
I proceeded to forget a multitude of so-called fundamentals and
worked solely on one thing—to learn to swing the clubhead
with my hands and let the rest of my anatomy follow the swing.

From that day on, not only did my golf improve to the extent that I was able to win the national championship, but I
learned that the game could be a joy and a pleasure, instead of
a mild form of torture, and an aggravation to a none too docile
temper.

For years, every time I missed a shot, I would immediately
take inventory of my well memorized list of fundamentals: Had
my elbows been in the proper position at the top of the swing?
Were my wrists cocked at the same point? Had my head remained stationary while the rest of my body turned, or hadn't I
pivoted enough; was my weight distributed correctly? Possibly
I had just turned my body too fast during the down swing. I
would try the next time to remember all of these things, and
perhaps, if I didn't die from brain fever, my next shot would be
a good one.

You can imagine what a pleasure it was to learn that all of this was unnecessary as it was impossible. I do not mean to say I promptly knew what swinging meant, not at all. I had as much difficulty as anyone making that jack knife in the handkerchief travel in an arc instead of figure eights. But once I could swing it, the sensation was such a delightful one I could hardly wait to get my club in my hands to swing it the same way. So much concentration was necessary to feel the clubhead swing, as I had felt the knife swinging, that I had not time to remember any list of fundamentals.

Besides, this was fun. I was getting a sense of controlling that clubhead, which was an entirely new experience. There is no sensation in golf quite so delightful as feeling the club-head swing. I have had days when I did swing the clubhead and consequently played very well, but I was not conscious of what I was doing, the result being, that the next day my shots might go wild, and I did not know quite how to straighten them.

If a slice had crept up on me, I could stop it by applying a little trick which, in a short while, would develop a hook and then I would be no better off than I was before, because I discovered that just as many trees, traps, and other hazards were waiting to catch hooks and slices.

Any tricks in golf can be exaggerated, and though it might cure a fault at first, when this happens it becomes a fault in it-self. Tricks are tempting because they are quick cures, and at first they give the impression that you have solved your problem, but I have served my time trying them. There is no trick to swing-ing the clubhead. It is definite action and not too quickly un-derstood and acquired. But anything that can add yardage and accuracy to my golf shots, and give me such a sense of control is well worth the time I have spent learning it.

The most amazing, as well as amusing thing about it to me is this: Since I have made a practice of forgetting fundamentals and tried only to learn to swing, professionals and good golfers have repeatedly told me how apparent these very fundamentals now are in my swing. This, above all else, has proven to me that the fundamentals of a golf swing, which are taught the world over, are undoubtedly correct, providing you forget them, learn to swing, and just allow them to happen.

All of this applies to my every day golf, and has meant a great deal to me, but the result it has had upon my tournament golf is not less important. Tournament golf is far more difficult because of the psychological factors involved. One is under a terrific mental strain, and a week of such strain pulls one down physically. When my mind was encumbered with many fundamentals, I found myself under great tension. One of some twenty things might cause a shot to be missed, and the natural tendency is to try to guard against them. No brain is capable of concentrating on more than one thing at a time, so when I discovered that swinging the clubhead was the one fundamental to concentrate on in order to possess the others, a large part of the metal disturbance was eliminated.

The first tournament I entered after adopting this method I won. It was the first time in my life I had been able to win a thirty-six-hole final. A weak back has been a handicap to me for years, and when I would tighten my muscles in an effort to keep my head still, my left arm straight, etc., the strain upon my back was too much. I would tire quickly and could not last thirty-six holes. By trying only to swing and allowing my body to follow that motion, as it naturally will if not forced to do otherwise, the strain ceased and I discovered that thirty-six holes were not difficult. I also discovered that I could practice three times as long without tiring.

The mental advantages proved just as great. Anyone who rode to the Wentworth Club with the American team on their way to play the International Team Match against Great Britain would never say that a top-class golfer has no nerves. Nervousness is shown in various ways, depending upon the temperament of the person. I do not know how many of the girls noticed this fact during that short ride, but it was apparent to me. Some were talking incessantly, others not saying a word, the majority of us were yawning, a true sign of nervousness, I dare say none of us were quite sure what we had eaten for breakfast.

There is no nervous strain in golf equal to playing an International Match. A true champion, regardless of whether her nervousness is apparent or otherwise, plays better golf under a strain. It rather keys one up for the battle. I have never enjoyed a match more than the foursome that morning. Miss Helen Hicks and I were paired against Miss Wilson and Mrs. Watson. Neither of us ever played better. It was a two-ball foursome, and when we finished the match on the seventeenth green we had a four for a 72 and had only won two and one.

In the singles that afternoon, I was paired against Miss Wanda Morgan, and I found myself three down at the end of nine holes, and two down going to thirteen. Here was a splendid opportunity to see if concentrating only on swinging would prove sufficient. I know that the best way to hit a golf ball is to concentrate on one thing. It worked, and I won two and one.

This last national championship in which I played the final against Miss Hicks was another test. I was four down on the fifteenth green, and I had to sink a 10-foot putt to keep from going five down. That putt dropped fortunately, and I ended the first eighteen holes only two holes behind. I still refused to concentrate on anything but swinging the clubhead, and, with my share of good fortune, managed to win the championship.

When any method proves itself so successful under two such circumstances, I am not inclined to cast it aside lightly. I shall never again try to do anything but swing the clubhead.

After Virginia Van Wie lost the United States Amateur to Glenna Collett two times in 1928 and 1930—the former loss by the biggest margin ever recorded—she determined thereafter to prove herself a champion. Despite a slender build, she perfected her game using the technique "swing the clubhead" (as explained above) by the great golf teacher, Ernest Jones. She went on to win, not just one United States Amateur Championship, but three—one of them against her friend and rival, Glenna Collett Vare.

II

Legends of the Fairway

The Early LPGA Years

"The pro circuit put 40,000 miles on my speedometer,
1,000 miles on my spiked shoes, and who knows how many
gray hairs under my sun visor."
Betty Hicks

An American Wins in Scotland

Babe Didrikson Zaharias
from *This Life I've Led*, 1955

Babe Didrikson Zaharias was not only considered a great golfer, but also the finest women athlete in the twentieth century. She had the strength and talent to compete in almost any sport—baseball, basket-ball, tennis, track, and she won three medals in the 1932 Los Angeles Olympics.

Her golf career began when the sportswriter Grantland Rice suggested they stop by a driving range one day. A year later, she won the 1935 Texas Women's Invitational. She won seventeen amateur tournaments in a row and was the first American to win the Ladies' British Open Amateur Championship in 1947—a championship she describes in the following essay. After that win, the lure of the sponsors and the fledgling LPGA convinced her to play as a professional. Babe went on to win thirty-one tournaments, including three United States Women's Open championships—one being the remarkable and emotional win at the 1954 Open at the Salem Country Club shortly after an operation for cancer. She lost her battle with cancer just two years later.

I got out early the morning of my first match in the Ladies' British Open Amateur Championship. I expected to see a crowd already gathering, the way it does for an American tournament. But there was hardly a soul in sight.

I said to the club secretary, "I thought Scotland was golf country. Where are all the people?"

He said, "They'll be here." And sure enough, all these buses began coming in, and by the time I teed off there must have been several thousand people there. They didn't come early because there was nothing for them to do at the course. They couldn't go to the clubhouse, naturally. Not even the golf pros were allowed in the clubhouse. I understand that's changing now at the British clubs. Anyway, there were no facilities for the spectators at Gullane, so the people didn't get there until it was time for the matches they wanted to see.

On the first tee there was a sign saying, "No Practice Swing." Well, I never hit practice balls off the tee when I'm about to play a match. If you don't hit one right, then immediately you start trying to correct your swing-and it's too late for that. The most I'll do is chip and putt a little bit before the start of a match.

But I do like my practice swing. It sort of gets me in the groove. Since it was against the rules in this tournament, I got in the habit of going off to one of the few spots where the grass was cropped down enough and taking my warm-up swings there. Then my match would be called, and when I got up on the first tee, I'd sometimes forget and automatically start to take another practice swing. But I always remembered in time and checked myself.

Anyhow, the starting time came for my first match, which was against a girl named Helen Nimmo. And I spotted these two little old Scotsmen sitting on a bench. They were wearing kilts. I'd gone to Scotland with the idea that all the men wore kilts, but I found that wasn't so around Gullane. These two were the first I'd seen. I asked about them later, and was told that they were golf professionals from the North Highlands, where the men do wear kilts right along.

Those two just fascinated me. They were in my galleries all through the tournament. They'd always be sitting on that bench near the first tee, and after my opponent and I drove off, they'd join the crowd and follow me around the course. They'd walk along with their heads close together, gabbing and gabbing, and those kilts would be bobbing up and down.

So my first match began, and I couldn't get over how quiet the gallery was. They were so orderly in moving around the course—there was none of the wild stampeding you sometimes have with American crowds. And they didn't yell or applaud. The most you'd hear would be somebody saying, "Well played," or "Fine shot."

I was saying to myself, "Gee, you have to knock the ball in the hole off the tee to get a hand around here." Well, I clinched that first match on the twelfth hole. And it wasn't until then that they all applauded.

I told Mrs. Helen Holm, a past Ladies's British Amateur champion, who was acting as a marshal, "I wish these people would just holler and enjoy themselves the way the crowds do back home." And she explained that the Scottish tradition was for the gallery to be very quiet so as not to disturb the players.

But I was going to loosen up those galleries if I could. In my match that afternoon I began kidding them a little. I said, "Come on, let's have some fun." I told them they could make all the noise they wanted to and it wouldn't bother me. I said the noise would make me play better, because it was what I was used to.

My opponent in the afternoon round was Mrs. Enid Sheppard. She gave me a pretty tough match, but I won it on the sixteenth hole, 4 and 2. When a match ends like that in an American tournament, we often go ahead and play out the rest of the course. We play the by-holes to give the crowd a little extra show.

I asked Mrs. Sheppard, and I asked Helen Holm, "Would it be all right to play the by-holes?" Mrs. Holm said at first the she didn't know whether we should, because that wasn't done in Scotland. But she's spent quite a bit of time in the United States herself, and finally she said to go ahead and do it.

I gave them some of the trick shots I use in exhibitions in this country. There's one where I put a kitchen match on the ground behind my ball on the tee, and when I drive, it sounds like a small cannon being fired, because that match goes off with a loud pop.

I did that off the seventeenth tee, and the ball sailed nearly 300 yards out there and landed in a trap right in front of the green. From the trap I did another of my stunts. I balance one ball on top of the other, which is quite a trick in itself. I swing, and the bottom ball is supposed to go on the green and the top one into my pocket. Well, not only did the one ball jump into my pocket, the other went right into the hole.

By this time the gallery was in an uproar. When I finished out on the eighteenth green by turning around backwards and putting the ball between my legs into the cup, they didn't quiet down for a long time. They kept me out there giving autographs for nearly an hour.

The next day there was a sign on the bulletin board: "Please do not play the by-holes." So I didn't do that anymore. But those crowds got bigger and friendlier every day. They sounded almost like the crowds at home by the end of the tournament.

One of the British golf writers, Fred Pignon, headed his story of that first day: OUR GIRLS SHAKEN BY GOLF 'BABE.' He wrote:

"Mrs. Zaharias took practically all the spectators and crashed her way over the hills and dales of this testing, undulating course. She tore holes in the rough with tremendous recovery shots, and simply bettered her opponents in both her matches with the most tremendous exhibition of long driving ever seen in women's golf."

There was just one person there that week who seemed to resent my coming over to try and win their championship. That was a woman whose name I've forgotten. She wasn't in the tournament herself, but I believe she was a former player. Well, all of us contestants had cards that admitted us to the clubhouse for tea. I went up there that first afternoon, and this woman invited me to join her.

Of course, I wanted to be friends with everybody, and I sat down with her. And she began telling me, "Did you know that there is a jinx against American women in this tournament? Why, your greatest players have come over here, women like Glenna Collett and Virginia Van Wie, and they've never been able to win."

I told her, "I didn't come over here to lose," and I broke away without making a scene. That was one woman who didn't speak my language, and I don't mean because of her Scottish accent.

In my two matches the next day I was really on my game. Women's par at Gullane was seventy-six, and men's par was seventy-one. At least, that's the way the experts calculated it. There was no official par for the course.

In the morning against Mrs. Val Reddan, I was even with the men's par through the first nine holes, and only one over it by the fourteenth, where I closed out the match, 6 and 4. In the afternoon I shot the first nine in 33—two under men's par. Mrs. Cosmo Galconer had a 40, which was only one over women's par, but she still was five down at the turn. The final score of that match was 6 and 5.

Both the other American girls were eliminated that day—
Helen Sigel in the morning and Ruth Woodward in the after-
noon. That left me as the only one with a chance to bring the
United States its first Ladies' British Amateur title.

Another of the differences I was having to get used to over
there was the Scottish caddies. They're elderly men—the one
I had looked about eighty years old to me. And they're accus-
tomed to giving the golfers a lot of advice about how to play.

I never take advice from a caddy, other than to ask them
about distances and directions if I'm not too familiar with the
course. I always plan my own shots and pick my own clubs.

Well, it wasn't long before this old fellow started in telling
me what he thought I should do. At first I said to myself, "I'll
just ignore him." But then we came to one shot where I wanted
to drop the ball on the green with my wedge. And the caddie
handed me a 3-iron.

I said, "Would you please leave the clubs in the bag and let
me pick them out?"

He said, "Madam, the wind is against you. You should take
this 3-iron and run the ball up there."

I told him, "I don't play 2 and 3-iron pitches on little short
shots. I'm used to hitting the ball up in the air." And I finally got
to play it my way with the wedge.

Later, there was a story that I went to the caddie master and
asked, "Don't you have any younger caddies here?" And he said,
"Yes, Mrs. Zaharias, we'll be glad to get you a younger boy." And
he brought out a caddie who was only seventy-five-years old.

Actually I kept my same caddie straight through the tournament. He stopped trying to choose my clubs for me after I
asked him not to, and carried my clubs in good style.

On the third day, a Wednesday, I was to play Frances Stephens in the quarterfinals in the morning. If I got by her, I

probably would face Jean Donald in the semifinals in the afternoon. That was the match they'd been making a big thing out of in the newspapers. Jean Donald was the Scottish girl who was supposed to have the best chance of beating me and keeping the championship at home.

They were talking it up around the club all week. People would say to me, "You and Jean Donald should have a wonderful match if you come up against each other. She's a fine golfer, and this is her home club. She really knows how to play this course.

Well, they didn't realize it, but that sort of talk just builds me up. The bigger they make a match, the more I get fired up to go out there and show them. It was like the year that the late O.B. Keeler, the well-known Atlanta golf writer, picked Louise Suggs of Atlanta to be the top woman golfer. That got me hustling so much that I had one of my very best years on the tournament circuit.

In the quarterfinals in the morning against Frances Stephens I had my hardest match. I shot men's par for the first nine holes—and she held me even. After thirteen holes I was still even with men's par—and only one up. But I took both the fourteenth hole by a stroke, and then I halved the sixteenth to win out, 3 and 2.

In the afternoon against Jean Donald—well, she's a nice girl and a nice golfer, but that wasn't her day. We had a real mob of people following us. The Associated Press account said,

"The crowd, attracted by the report that the Scottish champion was out to slay the American champion, grew to almost unmanageable proportions. Estimated by golf writers at between 5,000 and 8,000, the gallery was the largest of the season—far larger than the crowd which

gathered to watch the British men's amateur at Car-
noustie two weeks ago. Nearly one hundred stewards
barely preserved order."

Jean Donald was hitting her drives almost as far as mine for
a while, but I beat her with my short game. The match only
lasted thirteen holes, and I was one under men's par for as far as
we went. I had just one 3-putt green, and there were six times
when I was able to hole out with a single putt. It ended 7 and 5,
which is a runaway score in an eighteen-hole match.

Like any other woman, I'm forever freshening up my lipstick. Coming off the twelfth green I was putting new lipstick
on. I was just doing it automatically, not even thinking about
it. Well, it happened that I had her six down with six to play at
that time. One of the writers said in his story that I was so sure
I'd close out the match on the next hole I stopped to put lipstick on to get ready for the photographers.

The photographers swooped down after that next hole, all
right. Jean Donald was a real good sport about her defeat. She
posed with me dancing the Highland Fling and everything. I
had been over to her house for tea and dinner and stuff like that.
We had become very good friends. Her father was a doctor.

Another person I saw a lot of that week was the father of
Jimmy Thomson, one of our professional stars. Jimmy has always
been a great friend of mine in this country, and when he heard I
was going to Scotland he said to be sure and look up his dad at
the Berwick golf course. So I did. Jimmy's dad was the sportiest
looking guy in all of Scotland, wearing these sports jackets and
slacks that Jimmy had sent him from the United States.

He walked around with me in every match I played over
there. He looked just like Jimmy, and was the same wonderful kind of fellow. He kept talking to me in his Scottish burr,

"You're doing fine. You're a beautiful player." He really did a lot to keep me pepped up all through that tournament.

Meanwhile I kept running into that woman I mentioned earlier who tried to get me worried about the "jinx" against American players in the British Women's Amateur. She'd buttonhole me every time she saw me at the club or the hotel and say, "Don't forget about the jinx." Finally some of the other women found out what she was doing. They must have told her she was being unsporting, and to pipe down, because when I saw her in the clubhouse the last day, she just said, "Hello," and nothing more.

I'll have to admit I was thinking about the jinx a little bit the night before the final round. After all, I could get unlucky and have a bad day like anybody else. The girl I was going to play, Jacqueline Gordon, had been the big surprise of the tournament. She wasn't supposed to be one of the top British women players. She wasn't on their Curtis Cup team or anything. But she'd been beating everybody all week long.

I had my dinner down in the hotel dining room, and then went up to my room. They were still knocking themselves out to please me at that little inn. They were running low on bacon, and the chickens weren't laying quite so many eggs, but they still had plenty of the ham. And the maids had been instructed to take my golf clothes and socks and things and launder them whenever I asked. I can't tell you how grateful I felt to those people.

They had put a heater in my room for when it turned cold, and I needed it the night before the finals. I pulled down the blackout shades to keep out that late-evening light. But I couldn't sleep. Finally I got out of bed and put up the shade and sat by the window.

I ordered up some tea. It was brought by the little fellow who doubled as a desk clerk and bellboy and everything. I told him I was kind of upset, and that it was partly because of the unpleasant way that woman had been needling me about the jinx.

He said, "Mrs. Zaharias, don't take any notice to her. Everybody here wants you to win."

Eventually I did go to sleep. When I woke up it was a beautiful morning. Some of the other days the weather had been pretty mean. People thought it must be tough on me having to play under those conditions. Actually I was ready for it. Before leaving the United States, I'd gone out and practiced like mad every time there was bad weather, just to help prepare myself for this tournament on a Scottish seaside course.

The last morning, though, the weather was so lovely that I dressed in some of my warm-weather clothes. I put on a light skirt with a light sweater, and white golf shoes and white visor, I had a white golf glove with green backing to cover up that injured thumb on my left hand. Oh, I was a doll that morning, I'm telling you!

It was so nice and warm I didn't even bother to take along my siren suit and slacks, which I found out was a mistake. And I was having a little trouble with my golf shoes. I'd brought along a new pair of brown all-weather shoes that I'd had made especially for this trip, but they'd begun to split from getting wet so often out on the course, and then standing by the heater to dry. So I had to switch to an old pair of golf shoes for the final.

I got out there for my match with Jacqueline Gordon, and this time there already was a crowd waiting for us to start. I could still pick out those two little Scotsmen in kilts, though. I got up on the first tee and looked around, and I saw the British flag flying at the top of the flagpole. I stood at attention and saluted it. The crowd applauded.

Then I looked for an American flag, and someone pointed to the roof of the clubhouse. They had this big American flag stretched out there. I turned around and got right down on the ground and salaamed three times. Everybody roared.

So we started to play. Going down the first and second fairways, I waved as usual to everybody in those houses across the street. Only now it was mostly the servants and the children that I was waving to. The other people were at the tournament themselves.

We hadn't been out there long before the weather turned chilly and windy. Pretty soon I was wishing for my cold-weather stuff. All I had along with me in the golf bag was a blue sweater. I didn't burn up the course during that morning round the way I had in practically all my other matches. And Jacqueline Gordon was playing real good. She wasn't a long hitter, but she was consistent. At the twelfth hole she went two up. I squared it at the fifteenth, and we were still all even at lunchtime.

When I came off the course for the lunch break, fifty Scotsmen must have told me, "Babe, go git your slocks on. Go git your slocks on." I was going to do that, and I was also going to do something else.

I didn't waste any time getting back to the hotel after my morning round against Jacqueline Gordon in the finals of the British Women's Amateur. Along with getting some warmer clothes, I wanted to try and have my best golf shoes fixed to wear in the afternoon. These were the shoes that had cracked because of the dampness.

At the inn they served me a nice lunch in my room. Then I stretched out for a short rest. After a few minutes I got up and dressed. I put on my siren suit and slacks, which I'd failed to take with me during the morning. The newspapers said the next day that I switched to my "lucky slacks." But I didn't do it for the luck. I was just cold!

I headed for the shoemaker shop. I'd been told where it was, and also that it was a lady shoemaker. I got there, and she had a sign in her window like others I'd been seeing in shops along the way: "Sorry. Closed. Gone To See the Babe."

When I got to the clubhouse, somebody asked if I'd had my shoes taken care of, and I said, "No, she was closed." Well, somehow the word circulated through the crowd to the lady shoemaker. It wasn't but a few minutes later that she came up to me and said, "Did you have some shoes you wanted fixed?"

I said, "Yes, ma'am, I sure do." And she took my shoes back to her shop and repaired them, and brought them back to me before we teed off. It was such a nice thing for her to do.

I was really feeling good by the time Jacqueline Gordon and I started in again. I said to myself, "I just know I'm going to play a lot better now." I broke our tie on the very first hole in the afternoon. I got a par four and she had a five.

On the second hole, a par five, I had a long drive and then a long second shot that put me on the green. I holed out an eighteen-footer for an eagle three, which of course gave me the hole. When I won the third hole too, with a par five to her six, I knew for sure I was in charge.

Jacqueline Gordon hung in there, but things kept going my way. About the best she could do was to halve some of the holes. Those two kilted Scotsmen were still in my gallery, and gabbing away more excitedly than ever.

On one hole I hit a tremendous tee shot. I really creamed it. Oh, that drive felt good! It left me just a wedge shot to the green. Walking down the fairway, I was close enough to that pair in kilts to hear one of them saying to the other, "I've watched

Walter Hagen and Bobby Jones and Gene Sarazen and all those Americans who've played over here, and none of them could hit the ball better than this girl can."

Now that kind of talk is nice to hear. At this point I felt I just had to say something to them. I fell in step behind them and put my arms across their shoulders.

"How would you boys like to see me knock this little wedge shot right in the cup?" I said.

They said—I can't really do that Scotch burr—"Ah! That would be fine!" So I hit the ball, and it banked just a little bit, and stopped right on the edge of the cup. It almost did go in. And you should have seen the expressions on the faces of those two Scotsmen. Their mouths were hanging wide open.

I was five up going into the back nine. Jacqueline Gordon took the next one—it was the only I lost that afternoon. I won the hole after that. Then we played three straight halves, which ended the match, since I was five up and there were only four holes left.

The crowd gave me a wonderful ovation when it was over. It seemed like they stood for fifteen minutes and applauded. Then there was more picture-taking and dancing the Highland Fling and signing autographs and everything.

Finally there was the presentation of the championship trophy. I sang a little Highland song I'd learned from some of the Scottish golf pros in the United States—hoping I'd have this occasion to use it. Everybody seemed to like that touch.

Babe Zaharias believed there was no sport she could not conquer. Her determination to master golf would simply not be denied. She was known to hit 1,500 balls during each practice session, and she loved competitive games—always playing her best when the match was close.

She enjoyed the galleries and thrived on the energy they would bring to the round. It just wasn't any fun unless everybody was having fun, and she would often tell jokes, wisecrack with her golfing buddies, or play a tune on her beloved harmonica.

My Trip to Pine Valley

Helen Hicks
from "The American Golfer," 1932

Helen Hicks won the Canadian Ladies' Championship in 1929 and the United States Women's Amateur in 1931—where she defeated the unbeatable Glenna Collett Vare. Following her victory over Glenna—a rare occurrence in those days—a new generation of women golfers took notice of "Hard Hitting" Helen's swing and became considerably more aggressive.

In 1935 Helen became the first important women golfer to turn professional by signing with the Wilson Sporting Goods Company to promote their line of golf equipment for women. From then on women golfers began to earn money from sponsors as well as tournaments, and many golf clinics were set up as a way to promote the stars as well as the equipment.

Here Helen describes her adventures on Pine Valley in New Jersey, a course that is legendary for its beauty and its difficulty.

Pine Valley, the superlative golf course. I had heard of this famous creation of Mr. George Crump almost from the time I first began to play golf, down there in the wooded hills and valleys of southern New Jersey, a short way removed from Philadelphia. Many times I had had tentative engagements to visit and play it, but always something seems to have bobbed up to prevent me from doing so, that is until I made a visit to some friends at Princeton late last fall. During this stay, it was suggested that we take a day for a trip to this famous course, and I was, of course, all for it. I even lost some sleep the night before from thinking of the prospect, and planning how I would go about tackling it the next day.

Many tales had reached my ears about the difficulties of low scoring even for first flight players. But I had been playing well at the time, and frankly figured that no course was so difficult that, under favorable conditions, I could not break 90. My friends who had played there smiled as we framed some modest wagers that I would not do 90 or better.

Following a fifty-mile drive we reached the club, situated something like a mile off the main highway on a road that winds like a woodland path, past shining lakes. The clubhouse is lovely, but not pretentious, homey and comfortable with all modern appointments. In due time we were all ready for the start, and as we reached the first tee, I said to myself, "Well. Pine Valley at last!"

The first hole is a two-shotter, with a dogleg to the right. I hit a nice drive and followed with a spoon which got me home near the middle of the green, and two putts were enough to get down. "This looks easy enough," I thought to myself, though I didn't say anything. "All you have to do is hit the ball straight."

In that last statement I was entirely correct, but I was to find that you *must* hit it straight, and I didn't have to go any farther than the second hole to learn it. This is a three-shooter for women players, and I smashed out a good long drive, which, however, appeared to be possibly a foot too far to the right. A foot isn't much in matters of this sort, but it was plenty here. I was in trouble, and I mean *trouble*. By the time I eventually got that pesky ball in the hole I had taken seven strokes! A little of the self-assurance over that satisfactory par 4 on the first hole appeared to be escaping me.

Then when we turned to the short third, 175 yards in length, I realized immediately why they tell you that they never rake the traps at Pine Valley. An entire army would be needed for the job. For here was an expanse of sand at least fifty yards wide, stretching from the green back toward the tee. It was something distinctly new to me, something on the grand scale all right. Is it to be wondered that I failed to hit that green? I did.

The fourth calls for a blind tee shot with an open second, and it ought not to be terribly difficult, but it cost me a 6 against a par of 4 just the same. But my spirit rose somewhat when I hit a fine tee shot to the green of the 214-yard fifth, even though I did putt atrociously and take a 4 on the hole. This incidentally is one of the finest of one-shot holes, with elevated tee and green, having a lake between. One of my playing partners put a slight fade on his tee shot, and his ball wound up 25 yards down the slope in the woods, and the hole cost him a 7, several of which were vigorous licks with a niblick.

The sixth, calling for a well-placed tee shot and an accurate 2-iron to get home yielded no special thrills nor yet disasters for me, but the seventh! This is the longest looking golf hole I have ever seen. After what I considered an exceptionally fine drive, I took a brassie and hit the ball as well and as hard as I could, and it just managed to clear the far limit of a sand waste at least a hundred yards wide. My next effort was a full spade mashie which got me nothing more than a ball stuck in the sand of a deep trap in front of the green. By the time I finished my labors here I had another 7. Ugh!

By this time I was more than grateful for one of the few pars that were coming my way, that at the 8th. Whereas a slice or fade will lead you into the woods or a long deep trap, I managed to hit a straight drive and stick my second with a mashie-niblick on the postage-stamp green to get my 4.

At any rate by now, we were nearly half through. The ninth is not a particularly hard hole and two good shots will get home, but I happened to pull my drive off the line to the left, and the next thing I knew, I was digging and hewing my way out of the sand and underbrush. By the time I had played my fourth stroke on this hole, I realized that traps are *traps* at Pine Valley. Of course, I had been warned in this matter in advance, but I was foolish enough to figure that I knew how to recover from traps, and that a lot of this talk was just talk and nothing more. But I'll leave it to you to imagine some of the things that happened to me on that hole, when I tell you I holed a 20-foot putt for an 8!

Now we turned for home to face the tenth, a one-shotter calling for a spade mashie from the tee. The green is banked up at the back, but slopes away on three sides.

On the eleventh, the drive must be well-placed. Playing into the sun, I thought as my ball went on its way toward the green, I'd be putting for a 4 all right, but on finding the ball embedded in a trap that hole went a glimmering.

I experienced no strange or unusual adventures on the next three holes, although I narrowly averted trouble at the one-shot fourteenth where the tee shot is from a high elevation to a green flanked on three sides by water. My ball stopped just about a foot short of the water on the far edge of the green. But then came more humbling experiences at the fifteenth, another very long one. The drive must carry a lake; mine did so, but I still needed two more woods and a chip, as the route is all uphill and the way very narrow. But I made the mistake of pulling a brassie shot and had another session with the underbrush—and another 7 on my card.

With a wind back of me, and a high tee shot I got a 200-

yard carry at the sixteenth, and managed to get home a 3-iron second. Then a good drive and good 4-iron got me home at the seventeenth, where I finally managed to hole another par, one of the few of the round.

Standing on the eighteenth tee, somebody was inconsiderate enough total up the score to that point. It was evident that my bets had all gone wrong—I had taken an even 90 to there. But with at least a show at bravery, I asserted that I hadn't done so badly; that at least I had not taken double figures as yet, not even a 9. But there was still something in store for me. I found my drive on the high slope to the left of the fairway, and by the time I had finished my battling with the sand and rough, I just managed to get the ball down with my ninth stroke. I had done a 99! Well, anyhow I had broken 100.

But in spite of that bloated score I never enjoyed a round of golf more. Every hole is different from every other. Each one is a distinct adventure in itself.

There is nothing else like Pine Valley in golf in this country; it is a golfer's paradise. Naturally I was disappointed in my score, but I did get a bit of satisfaction later. I played another round. This time I finished out with a 90, which included no less than seven 3-putt greens. Not a brilliant score by any means, but at least an improvement over that first experience.

In 1932, Helen Hicks played in the first Curtis Cup match—a match between Great Britain and America played every other year. The first Curtis Cup match was a one-day event consisting of three foursome matches and six single matches. One point was awarded for each victory and half a point for halved matches. Helen contributed a point by winning one of the foursome matches with her partner Virginia Van Wie. Together they shot a 68 for 17 holes and beat the famous Enid Wilson and Mrs. J. B. Watson, 2 and 1. America won 5½ to 3½ points.

"You're Always Learning New Ideas, New Methods. It Keeps You Young."

Patty Berg

from *Gettin' to the Dance Floor*, 1986

The pride of Minnesota, redheaded and quick-witted Patty Berg won the 1934 Minneapolis City Ladies' Championship just three years after she took up the game of golf—she was just sixteen years old. A year later she made it to the finals of the United States Women's Amateur Championship in her hometown of Minneapolis, but lost to the great Glenna Collett Vare in the final (ironically, she was a three-time winner of the Vare Trophy).

After over thirty amateur championship wins, Patty turned professional in 1940, joining a new breed of American women golfers, but her career was interrupted because of a knee injury sustained in a car crash. When she was able to resume her golfing career, she was elected first president to the newly formed LPGA. She won fifty-seven professional (three as an amateur) tournament titles, including fifteen major victories, and was one the four original inductees into the LPGA Hall of Fame in 1951. Here she discusses her career in an interview with the famous golf writer Al Barkow.

When I was a little child living in Minneapolis, about seven doors down from me lived a fellow by the name of Charles "Bud" Wilkinson. He was a guard on the University of Minnesota football team, and in his last year was the quarterback. So anything he did, I had to do. We had a football team called the 50ᵗʰ Street Tigers. Bud was the guard, coach, and captain, and I was the quarterback because I was the only one who could remember the signals. We had one—22—and when I yelled it out everyone ran whichever way they wanted. Well, Bud finally told me I had to quit because I was too slow and short and there wasn't any future in it for me.

So I went into speed skating, and did a lot of that. I skated in the national junior championships, intermediate division, and in the state championships; won some medals, too. Then there was a time when we were skating in some little town in Minnesota and, oh, it was cold. I remember coming to the finishing line going so fast I ended up in one of the drifts, and my dad came over and said, "Well, your mother and I are going to Florida tomorrow," and I told them to wait for me.

I was about twelve years old when I started swinging a club. I would swing away in the backyard, and my father was always wondering who was taking the divots—see, my sisters also played a little golf. Well, Dad caught me out there one day knocking up the grass and said, "How would you like to get that clubhead in the back of a golf ball?" I said I'd like that, and that's when it really began. We were members at the Interlachen Country Club, which was where Bobby Jones won one of his Grand Slam championships in 1930—the U.S. Open. I wasn't there for that. I was in 6B at John Brown's Elementary School at the time, running in a track meet—won the thirty-yard dash.

Anyway, I took my first lessons at Interlachen from Willie Kidd, the head professional, and Jim Pringle, his assistant. But then for about forty years I took lessons from Lester Bolstead, who was the golf professional at the University of Minnesota. He coached the men's golf team at the university. His team won the Big Ten championship one year, which was quite something to do in Minnesota. He was a real taskmaster with me. He would stand there and say, "Now Patricia Jane, Patricia Jane"—he never called me Patty—"you've got to strive for perfection, you must conquer you flaws, you must use your legs." And every time he said my name he would clap his hands: "Patricia Jane," clap, "Patricia Jane," clap. But he is a great golf professional and a very knowledgeable man. He knows so much about anatomy, and uses that in his teaching.

I won the 1934 Minneapolis City Ladies' Championship, which was the most memorable event in my golf career because I probably wouldn't had had a golf career if not for what happened. I played in my first City Ladies' championship the year before, when I was fifteen, and shot 122. That qualified me for the last flight, and in my first match some lady beat me on just about every hole. After that defeat I walked back to the clubhouse and said to myself, "I'm going to spend the next 365 days trying to improve." For the next year, all I did was eat, sleep, and play golf. I thought if I could move up a flight or shoot better than 122, that would be an improvement. Well, 365 days later I was medalist and won the Minneapolis City Ladies' Championship.

It's very possible that if I didn't improve on my 122, or didn't move up a flight or so, I might not be in golf today. But I didn't think I'd win that tournament. When I did, I started to dream. I thought, maybe I'll be able to play the Minnesota State Women's Championship; maybe I'll be able to play in some of the tournaments in Florida, maybe even play in the Trans-Mississippi and the Women's Western Amateur and the United States Women's Amateur. I really started to dream that golf was my future, and that's exactly how it turned out.

That's a long time to spend on one endeavor, isn't it—365 days? But I'll tell you, it was worth every freckle on my face. What did I learn during that time? To hit the ball straighter by improving my tempo, timing, and rhythm. I got to know more about the swing, so I could correct myself during a round—you know, you're quarterback out there. And I spent a lot of time chipping and putting, because I knew I wasn't going to hit all the greens—no one does—especially when you were as small as I was.

Of course, we had a short golf season up in Minnesota. If we were lucky, we would start playing in the first part of May. But a lot of times we'd play through October and November. If I made any swing changes at all, it was in October and November, because by the time we could play in the spring there wasn't time for that; the tournaments started coming up. I'd hit balls into a canvas, indoors, and in 1935 my family started going to Florida for a good bit of the winter. I spent a month in Florida the winter of '35, and that helped a lot in my winning the Minnesota State Women's Golf Championship and getting to the finals of the USGA Women's Amateur Championship. I would make up the schooling I missed, and when I made the U.S. Curtis Cup team in my last year of high school I was gone so much that my dad got a tutor for me.

My father had a grain company, H.L. Berg Company. He was a member of the Chicago Board of Trade, the Minneapolis Board of Trade, and the Winnipeg Board of Trade. He was a businessman golfer, and had a ten handicap. My brother was a fine player; he played in the city league and state championships.

But he had scarlet fever when he was a boy that left him with a bad heart, and he died at forty-three.

I went two years to the University of Minnesota, but didn't play golf for the school. There was just a men's golf team. But after I won that city championship my father sent me to tournaments. I played in the Minnesota State, of course, then the Trans-Miss, which was my first major event. I qualified for the championship flight and got beat by Opal Hill in the second round. But I did win the driving contest. I won a beautiful mirror. Then, in 1935 I was runner-up to Glenna Vare in the Women's National Amateur. In 1937 I was runner-up in just about everything, and somebody wrote an article calling me the uncrowned champion. But in 1938 I turned it all around and won ten out of thirteen tournaments.

I played amateur golf for part of 1939. Then, while I was on my way to defend one of my championships and having a wonderful year, I had an emergency appendectomy and was in the hospital for almost a month with a private nurse. I was finished for the season, so in September I took a trip for the University of Minnesota to raise funds. What I did was play in exhibitions that we wouldn't charge anything for, but at night we'd have dinners and raise money for the Student Union Building. We went out into the Dakotas and Montana and California, about eight or nine states, contacting alumni. That's when I played Pebble Beach for the first time, and met Bing Crosby and Richard Arlen. And Helen Langfeld, who has done so much for women's golf. She put on a lot of golf tournaments, including one for the LPGA, and does to this day at age eighty-five. A lot of the girls on the tour today played in Helen Langfeld's junior tournaments in California.

After I got back from that trip I went to college for another year, then in 1940 I turned pro. I went with the Wilson Sporting

Goods Company. They offered me a job, and it was a very good arrangement. My father went to Chicago and discussed it with Mr. Icely, the president of Wilson. You know, at that time you didn't have any managers, so your father was your manager, or at least helped you. My father was the greatest.

I wasn't the first woman pro, though. There were several before me, including Helen Hicks and Bessie Finn. Bessie became the pro at the Breakers in Palm Beach, where she succeeded her dad. She taught, but I think did mostly administrative work. Then there was Helen Dettweiler, Opal Hill, Hope Seignious. When I first turned pro, I think there were something like three tournaments—the Western Open, the Title Holders, and maybe the Asheville Invitational. Sometimes some other tournament would come along. The total prize money was about $500, and we had a field sometimes of only five players, plus outstanding women amateur golfers.

So we gave a lot of clinics for Wilson. I was used to doing the clinics, and learned how to do it during the eight years I played amateur golf. My father had me play around the state of Minnesota giving little clinics and exhibitions on weekends for different charities. A pro would give the instruction, while I hit the balls. Of course, I listened to how the pro made his presentation and picked up the technique that way.

What tour there was we did by train, or bus, or car, and in 1941 I had a terrible accident going from Corsicana, Texas, to Memphis. This was actually to play an exhibition for British War Relief. I was on the passenger side of the car, Helen Dettweiler was driving. Somebody hit us and I went into the dashboard and broke my left knee in three places. And, of course, my face hit the windshield—no seat belts in those days. Well, I was laid up for eighteen months and when they took the cast off I couldn't get the leg bent because of the adhesions. The knee started to turn blue, so they gave me gas and ether and hit it, or manipulated it. They did that twice, and I fell once, so I ended up with about seventy-five percent use of the leg on terms of bending it.

When I got out of the hospital, I went down to Mobile, Alabama, and took a training program with a prize fighter named Tommy Littleton, who had a gym down there. I rode a bicycle and did two hours of gym work a day with Tommy Littleton, and I got so I could hit golf balls, then so I could pick them up, and then finally so I could play. The first thing I did after that was play an exhibition at George S. May's Tam O'Shanter Country Club in Chicago. He had a nice luncheon for me, and I played and shot 78 from the men's tees. The course was playing long because it had rained a lot, so I thought I was back.

The doctors think now that maybe my hip was displaced a little from the accident and I didn't know it, and I walked for thirty-nine years with it that way. The doctors now ask me if I ever felt the displacement, or the pain, and I said I didn't. But I guess after a while you don't feel pain. Of course, in 1980 I had a total hip operation, I have an artificial left hip now. And in 1971 I had a battle with cancer. I had a massive tumor close to the kidney. But I'm fine now.

I joined the Marine Corps during World War II, and was an officer. I went to Camp LeJeune for officer's training, then to Philadelphia and worked in public relations and recruiting. I went in the service in 1943 and came out in 1945.

In 1946 we had an organization called the Women's Professional Golf Association. Later, Babe Zaharias and her husband, George, Fred Corcoran, and I reorganized it into the Ladies Professional Golf Association, which is the LPGA of today. In January 1948 we met at the Venetian Hotel in Miami. We wanted to get more tournaments to play, and that was Fred

Corcorans's job. He had been the PGA tour manager and knew everybody in the game. But the first thing we did was change the name from Women's to Ladies' Professional Golf Association. Fred thought it would be better to be ladies than women.

Then Wilson Sporting Goods gave us money for six years, not for prize money but for administrative purposes and to pay Fred Corcoran and his expenses. He was paid quite a bit of money for that time, but he did a good job. Then other manufacturers put in some money, and, well, it just grew and grew. It was so hard to envision then that women would be playing for $9 million in purses, as they are now.

The Babe—Zaharias—was a tremendous asset in the early days of the ladies tour. She starred in the 1932 Olympics and people wanted to come out and see her play golf. She was a household name. She gave them a show, too—a great competitor, a great player, and fun. I remember the time we played the British Walker Cup team in England. In the morning matches Babe and I lost to Davenport and a fellow named Beck; Betsy Rawls and Peggy Bush lost, too. But Peggy Kirk and Betty Jameson tied their match, so we're behind two points to a half-point. We're sitting around the table at lunch, with all the little American flags on it, and I said, "All of those who expect to win their singles, follow me." Babe says, "Come on, follow Napoleon." Anyway, we went out and all won our singles matches and beat them, six to two. Babe played Leonard Crawley, the golf writer. Leonard had a big mustache, and before they teed off Babe said to him, "If I beat you, do I get to cut your mustache off?" Leonard said, "You sure do." So after Babe beat him that afternoon she was running around the parking lot with scissors, trying to catch Crawley. She never did.

People have said that the Babe was a little crude once in a while, but I didn't see that in her. No, I saw a wonderful athlete and someone with a lot of class. I remember when she was suffering from cancer so badly, she'd tell everybody it wasn't so bad, we're all going to get better. She knew she didn't have a chance, but she went around to hospitals telling patients they were going to get better, and so was she. You think that's a lady with class? Yes, sir. She gave everybody hope.

I guess a woman athlete in my younger days had to deal with the tomboy image a little more than nowadays, but I never got ragged for being an athlete. I had a tremendous amount of support from everybody. I never had any problem with that, whatsoever. And the men pros always welcomed us with open arms when we played a tournament or gave a clinic at their clubs. In fact, I would get a lot of good instruction from some of the men. Johnny Revolta had a magnificent short game, and I took a lot of lessons from him whenever I was around Chicago during the summer, or out in California. Sam Snead helped me a lot. I think he's a marvelous teacher. He has a keen eye, and I always liked the way he rolled in with his left foot; that movement he did with his feet and ankles was terrific. But I'm not tall—only five feet two—so I had to swing like Gene Sarazen, who was a terrific competitor and player. I watched him a lot.

But if there is one thing I would tell all golfers about technique, it would be that the grip has a tendency to change even during the course of a round and you have to keep checking it day in and day out. The grip is the foundation of the swing. Well, there's another thing. You must work constantly on timing and tempo. You know, some days you just cannot do anything with your tempo—it gets too fast sometimes. Besides, I tend to do everything quickly because that's my nature. So if I got too fast and didn't complete my backswing, I'd just swing the club with my left hand—practice swing—then, without stopping, put my right hand on the club. That's how I'd get my tempo back. You see players on the tour doing this all the time, trying to get their tempo back; it's the best way I know to do it.

I guess there's one more thing I've learned about this game. I remember Bob Jones saying that no one could ever conquer golf, because it has so much to do with the nervous system. The big thing about this is you stand up there and you're hitting it just super and you start hitting it harder and harder, and pretty soon you're beyond your hitting capacity. You end up losing your timing and tempo, and have to start all over again. But there's always something to learn about this game. A lot of professionals, after playing a lot of years, decide to change their swing, make it more upright or flatter or something. You're always learning new ideas, new methods. It keeps you young.

In the beginning of my career, it was ninety-nine percent clinics and one percent tournaments for me, then it turned around to where it was eighty-five—fifteen in favor of tournaments. Now I'm back to where it's 100 percent clinics or golf shows, due to my hip problem. I can't play on the tour anymore, but I still give a lot of golf shows. Last year I gave over forty.

Putting

Patty Berg
from *Golf,* 1941

I sometimes feel that it doesn't matter how you play a putt, as long as the ball comes to rest in the cup.

I have had days when the putts seemed to roll in from any position, angle, or distance, with no special application on my part. On other occasions, the ball just won't go down," regardless of method or amount of concentration employed.

However, I do believe that if you are to be fairly effective at putting, you must observe certain fundamentals of stroking the ball.

I have observed that many of the top-flight professionals vary in putting methods, but usually have some common factors such as grip and the position of the ball.

Think of putting as a "game within a game." No matter how well you may be functioning in other departments of your game, if your putter is not "working," you cannot score well. On the other hand, you may play rounds when your tee, fairway, trap, or approach shots are not effective, but if your putts are dropping, you will come in with a low score.

I have experienced matches in which throughout the first nine holes, or so, I just couldn't sink a reasonably short putt. Then, as if by magic, they began to roll in from nearly every position on the green.

It seems to me that some golfers are naturally gifted putters, endowed from the very beginning with a fine stroke which has given them confidence. Confidence is an extremely valuable asset in putting.

While participating in my first National Women's Amateur golf tournament I had the good fortune to be putting with deadly effect. In fact, it was this department of my game which carried me through to the finals. I began to think that I was a "natural" putter, but subsequent relapses on the putting green dispelled this idea. I have since spent as much time in practicing with my putter as with any other club.

I have experimented extensively, changing grip, stance, and the position of the ball. I have solicited the suggestions of those prominent amateurs and professionals who are particularly noted for their putting methods. I have incorporated some of these ideas into my putting methods. Though still far from perfect, I do feel that I am now at least quite consistent in putting.

The following case-example shows an effective method of keeping a mental record of your putting, and also your other strokes. My home course, the Interlachen Club in Minneapolis, has an outgoing nine which includes four short par 4 holes, two par 3 holes, two short par 5 holes, and one fairly long par 5 hole. Par for men is 37 strokes. The incoming nine is comprised of two par 3 holes, two short par 4's, three long par 4's and two fairly long par 5 holes or a total par of 36.

I figure that if I hit my shots perfectly, I should play onto the greens on the first nine holes with 20 shots. If I use the regulation number of putts on each green (two) I should have a score of 38. On the last nine, which is longer, I should require 21 shots to get on the greens, and another 18 putts, for a total of 39 strokes, and 77 for the 18 holes.

Actually, it is difficult for me to reach the 18 greens in any less than 42 to 44 shots. Obviously, if I am to score near par of 73, I must use 32 putts, or less. I suggest you adopt this method as an interesting way to reveal your weaknesses and generally analyze your game.

Confidence played a great part in Patty's short game. On the green, for instance, she always believed that her ball would go in the cup after she struck it. She teaches that there are three things that everyone needs in the game of golf: to continue to work hard on your game, to keep swinging until you can repeat it consistently, and to determine that you must make one less mistake each time you play.

The Spirit of Being an Amateur

Betty Hicks

From *Liberty* magazine, July, 1942

Betty Hicks, while compiling an enviable record in women's golf, wrote over three hundred magazine articles for such prestigious publications as The Saturday Evening Post, Golf Digest, *and* Look. *She won the United States Women's Amateur Championship in 1941 and was twice runner-up to Babe Didrickson Zaharias in the United States Women's Open Championship (in 1948 and 1954). In 1944, together with founders Hope Seignious and Ellen Griffin, she started the Women's Professional Golf Association; the first national organization for women's professional golf and the predecessor of the current LPGA.*

After her retirement from professional golf, Betty became an avid golf-instructor and was awarded an honorary lifetime membership by the LPGA Teaching Division. In 1996 she coauthored, with her good friend Patty Sheehan, the book Patty Sheehan on Golf.

One March day of 1941 Dot Kirby shook hands with me on a Florida West Coast golf course and said, "Congratulations!"

My reply was a quiet "Thank you." But my tired nerves wanted to shout for me, "Thanks, Dotty! I'm sorry I had to get so preoccupied today, banging those birdie putts, knocking irons dead to the pin from out of the trees. An 8 and 6 beating isn't sweet to take, especially when you must know, as I know, that you're just as good a golfer as I am. But aren't you glad it's all over! I feel better already. Those knots in my nerves are all untied, and that sick, weak feeling is gone from my stomach. My month seems a little less like July in Death Valley now, too, and once in a while I can swallow to ease the pain in my throat. But this is the Big Time, Dotty, and I had to play this final match if it killed me. Tonight we will drive to Augusta for the next tournament, and tomorrow everyone will have forgotten Belleair, except you and me and perhaps those two boys who carried our clubs."

No, I really didn't have to play tournament golf that way. No one forced me into it. But it all started back in 1938.

Larry Gleason was a good pro. I remember the first lesson I took from him in the fall of 1937—how I learned to pivot, and how silly I thought it was when he called some of my shots "beautiful." Nothing in golf was beautiful to me then.

I couldn't understand, either, why he was so thrilled when I shot a 96 my first eighteen holes. Nor could I see why I should practice a game so apparently simple as golf. But Larry said it had to be. So I practiced. And the scores kept coming down, from that 96 in October to 86 the next April, 78 in May, and 75 the next August.

In October of 1938 I won my first tournament, the Long Beach City Championship. Perhaps it was then I began to wonder. Somebody game me a trophy cup. People slapped me on the back and said "Great going!" My picture was in the paper with a story about the match, making me feel that perhaps my golf shots *were* important. But the next day everyone seemed to have forgotten about it.

I didn't understand why I had worked so hard just for winning, when victory was so evanescent. "Larry, where is the going to get me?" I asked. "You told me to practice. And I have practiced, hours every day, when there have been other things I would rather have been doing. Then you told me I should play in tournaments. That was for experience. But that cost money. And what have I when I have experience? I would just like to know what this golf game will bring me before I put any more effort into it."

My tournament record for the three years which followed was to prove that my teacher had not been passing out idle encouragement when he answered, "I think that within a few years you will be among the top ten amateur women golfers in the country." But when he predicted, "And that alone will bring you fame and money," he destroyed most of the true spirit of amateurism I might have had, and replaced it with a desire for something more material—like headlines, pro contracts, convertibles, and winters on the Florida circuit.

So from that day on I played the game not entirely for the fame's sake but because I thought some magic golden gates would open.

Larry Gleason could have told me, "You play this game because—well, because you like the thrill of good shots, I suppose. And you like the feel of green grass under your feet. You like to practice in the evening, when you can laugh at the funny long shadow of your swing moving across the tee. You play golf, too, because it's a social game—you meet people and make friends. And you'll play it for all these things all your life, instead of for just a few fevered years. The more you put into golf that way, the more dividends it will pay you. Play when you want to play.

Practice when you feel like practicing. And enter tournaments you know you will enjoy, not for the exhilaration of winning but just to play the game."

But if he had told me that, I would never have been national champion.

Perhaps I have no sense of values now, but I'm certain that I had none then. I determined to pursue the golfing glory road as no girl had ever pursued it. If Patty Berg practiced six hours a day, I would practice eight. If Dorothy Kirby played in ten tournaments a year, I would play in twelve. If there was only one way to the top, I would take it.

Technically, I was an amateur, of course. I read the rules pertaining to Simon-purism and followed them. I did play golf because I liked it, or perhaps because it fascinated me so. But if I had played only when I like to play, I wouldn't be writing this.

By spring of 1939 I had begun to believe that California was a waste of time for an aspiring young golfer. Because I was eighteen, outspoken, determined, and hotheaded, I made some unpardonable *faux pas*.

"Condolences, Elizabeth," the mother of one of my victorious opponents said to me late in 1938. I came back with one of my worst replies. "Thanks, but you'd better save your condolences. You'll need them for your daughter next time I play her." I guess I forgot to smile when I said it.

Californians didn't like the way I made no pretense about wanting to win. They told me, "People like that will-to-win stuff in the East, but after all, it's only a game." I guess they had never thought of anything like those golden gates of mine, the ones opening toward "fame and money." So I didn't tell them about that. But I did go East in the summer of 1939.

Larry said before I went, "Find out how those girls back there are financed. Not all of them are wealthy. They must be getting boosts somewhere that are within the amateur rulings."

I found that out, but I discovered, too, very suddenly one August morning in Connecticut, that I was becoming a golfer. The New York papers had headlines about my victory in the national quarter-final over someone named Orcutt. It was supposed to have been an upset. I thought this was all rather strange, because I hadn't read the sports pages much. No one had told me Maureen Orcutt was good. I didn't know I was supposed to lose to her, so I went out and won. The papers said a Kirby-Hicks final would be popular, too. So I thought I maybe I should try a little harder against Betty Jameson in the semifinal. However, there were lumps in my throat then, my hands went cold and numb. Betty Jameson became national champion.

A month later Marion Miley and I were sipping Cokes in an Evanston, Illinois, drugstore after the final round of the Women's Western Derby. Suddenly I exclaimed, as though I had just awakened from a dream, "Well I'll be darned! I've won a golf tournament!" Marion laughed and said, "Of course you have. You've won the biggest medal-play tournament in the country."

I hadn't had nerves to trouble me in that tournament. Dot Kirby had gone into the last round with a one-stroke lead, but I don't believe I'd given it a thought. I'd shot a 73 for a tournament record total of 307 and beaten Dot by nine strokes. I had become a golfer!

I returned to California full of hope of easy years ahead, and I reported to Larry that some of the golfers had oil company jobs. "They just play golf with the customers and get new contracts. It's coincidental, maybe, but they have plenty of time for tournaments. There are a couple who work in the sports clothes department stores, and there are some with newspaper jobs—at good pay too." I told Larry that if I could get a job of some sort to finance more tournaments and more experience, I'll win the big one someday."

But, strangely enough, Californians don't feel that they owe their golfers a living. When I got home, they stuck the Derby cup in the clubhouse storeroom and forgot about it.

I was ranked No. 5 nationally in 1939. I thought the chamber of commerce or an oil company or some sportswear store would rush to me with a job. But they all overlooked it somehow.

So, I left California again in January of 1940 with Clara Callender, a former state champion who also had sadly discovered that you can't shake money off trees just by beating around the roots with a mashie. We drove South together with $250 each and big ideas about how to rip the Florida circuit apart.

I had learned a great deal in the Eastern events, principally not to fear the big-name stars. I wanted another crack at Betty Jameson, a chance to play Patty Berg. I would show the Californians that determination and zeal for perfection would win golf tournaments.

We played at Punta Gorda and the Miami-Biltmore first, and I was beaten on extra holes in both tournaments. My pride was sadly shaken. "Clara, I'm not going home until I win two down here," I announced. The fact that we had spent half our money didn't seem to matter. Clara couldn't say anything by O.K.—I owned the car.

I did win the next two. I defeated Betty Jameson at Palm

Beach in the semifinal, and the next day won from Grace
Amory for the championship. A week later, at Ormond Beach,
a freckle-faced golfing machine missed an eight-foot putt on
the first extra hole, and I had beaten Patty Berg in the semifinal.
Then I whipped Betty Jameson again, 3 and 2, for the South
Atlantic title.

They were good wins, but I also learned the mental pain of
being four down and eight to go, against Patty Berg. I learned
the feeling of whipping a tired swing into perfect effort on extra
holes. I learned to cry inwardly, "Why can't this be over!" I ate
breakfasts from which my nerves had torn all taste.

They were expensive wins, too. After Ormond Beach we
went to St. Augustine. Patty beat us both there, and we counted
our remaining assets. I had $1.45. Clara had very little more.

We returned to California on $20 contributed by one of
our charitable opponents. We were welcomed at the city lim-
its and escorted to the city hall, where we were congratulated
by the mayor. During the weeks that followed we were guests
at luncheon clubs. Chamber of commerce officials made long
speeches about how many thousands of dollars' worth of publicity we had brought to the city. Everybody thought it was very
funny how I had two cents when we got home and Clara, the
plutocrat, had three. And they would stick out their chests and
grin when we would say that Florida couldn't hold a candle to
California.

Larry said we'd get some jobs now. But the city publicity
bureau just went on pasting our press items in its scrapbook,
and dad kept on writing checks for me. I went to work on the
practice tee, with dreams of my arms around the national championship cup that September. I set up a grueling schedule for
myself. Every morning at eight I would go to the course, my
back still weary from the grind of the day before, my hands blis-

tered, my concentration wearied. I would be much better that summer, of that I was sure.

But I wasn't. I quick-hooked from Long Beach to Chicago, up to Detroit, down to Cleveland, then back home again and up to Seattle. An unassuming young woman from Portland climaxed the season for me by beating me 3 and 1 in the National second round. She left me standing on a cliff just off the eighteenth tee at Pebble Beach, hitting all my golf balls into the Pacific, vowing I would never play the horrible game again.

But I neglected to throw my clubs in too, so I was back again at it in a week, with a new pro and new determination. Olin Dutra, a former national champion, worked a couple of kinks out of my swing and I was off to the wars once more.

My swing had improved and shot-making was easier. But sleep was no quicker coming when there were tough matches the next day. I found no cause for happiness, either, in the fact that I was medalist in eight of the next ten tournaments in which I played, with an average of slightly under 76, and won four of them. Four I thought wasn't enough.

One of those four was the California State Championship, which I won in the spring of '41. It had eluded me before, probably because there are half a dozen girls in California who are as good as I am, though I wouldn't admit it to myself.

It was a sloppy win, though. Fate guided my ball around stymies when I was 3 down and 6 to go, and my accommodating opponents seemed to miss their shots at the most critical points in the matches. It left me figuring the price of the three years before—$8,000 for expenses; eight hours a day chasing a glory mirage which I could see but never reach; an inestimable damage in strain—physical, mental, and emotional.

I was tired of marking time on the glory road, stuffing good years down this beautiful but very blind alley. Frank

Newell, my husband, proved much more attractive than the fairest fairway or most sparkling silver prize in the country. Housekeeping didn't hurt my golf. But glandular fever did. Maybe it was the sulfathiazole I had to take that knocked my scores back into the 80s, or perhaps it was the three weeks I spent in bed. So I didn't even bother to count down to my name in the list of finishers in the Western Derby. I recall with a shudder four rounds of 82-87-75-89. At the time, I was too discouraged to be mad.

I don't know why anyone wanted me to give a driving-range demonstration after that, but I did it, and thereby I met a man named Allen. Mr. Allen, it seemed, was looking for a woman pro for the Dubow Company—just a top golfer whose name they could put on a line of clubs. Was I interested? After I was very unexcitingly removed from the Western Amateur Championship in the third round, it seemed to me a question of whether or not Dubow would still be interested. They still were.

"Do you want to sign the contract now?" they asked. I did. It was good offer, involving no traveling, no required exhibitions or demonstrations, and was financially very attractive.

"But I think," I said to them, "as long as I'm back here, I'll hop up to Boston and play in the National. I'll be back after a couple of rounds probably, and will take care of the contract then." The tragedy was that I believed it.

Two weeks later I went into something like the half-consciousness of a beautiful nightmare. When I awoke they were putting a big cup in my arms. I was national amateur champion!

Would I turn pro? The reporters asked. I said, "Of course I'll be receptive to offers." Perhaps my answer was too blunt and sincere. I should have said more so everyone would understand how I felt. I should have answered:

"So I'm national amateur champion. Sure, it's all very exciting. That semifinal with Estelle Page was the greatest thrill I've ever had. But even if I am the champ, so what? Who cares, really? Girls have been winning this tournament since the 1890s, so that's nothing new. It doesn't even prove that I'm the best golfer in the country, because all I did this week was put six rounds in the right places. The golfing gods were very kind to me. It sounds like I'm cashing in if I turn pro, doesn't it? But do you think I've played all this time for fun? I've had fun, of course. I wouldn't have missed it. But I've sacrificed more than I have received in return, I think."

I'm not going to make a great deal of money as a pro in the next few years. The steel that would go into golf clubs bearing my name will be bombing Tokyo, defending Australia in the war. But I certainly can't complain. There are bigger games than golf.

You ask me if I shall have any regrets. How should I know now? If I have, I'll discover them within the next few months. And then I'll be back to tell you about it.

I signed a professional contract in November. Not since the National have I played in a tournament. Now I play golf when and with whom I want to, and on courses of my choice. I stay home when it rains. I find practice rather tedious, so I rarely practice. I get some bad rounds as a consequence, but they are no longer any cause for worry. And good rounds are satisfying in themselves, not as means to an end.

The United States Golf Association won't agree with me, but I think I'm a better amateur—better golfer for the love of it—now than I was when I won the national championship. Professionalism has taught me that amateurism isn't something that can be written into rule books. It is the spirit in which you play the game.

Betty Hick's favorite swing checkpoint is to see that the toe of the club-head is pointing skyward at the midway (waist-high) points of both her backswing and her follow-through. She teaches that, "On the back-swing, the clubface position assures me of the proper action of arms, wrists, and hands in the swing and increases my chances of bringing the face into the ball square. On the follow-through, moving the clubhead into a toe-skyward position means I won't roll the face with a resultant hook. Nor will I open the face too much, with consequent slices, pushes, and shanks."

It's All in Your Head

Louise Suggs
from *Golf for Women*, 1953

Louise Suggs began playing golf at the age of ten on a golf course her father designed and built in their hometown of Lithia Springs, Georgia. She developed into a fine player and won the 1947 United States Women's Amateur and the 1948 Ladies' British Open Amateur—only the second American to do so. During her rookie year as a professional, Louise won the United States Women's Open by a record fourteen strokes over Babe Didrikson Zaharias.

In the early days of the LPGA, Louise was often matched with "the Babe" and Patty Berg. She described those events as "like watching three cats fighting over a plate of fish." In spite of, or perhaps because of the competition among the three of them, Louise had her best years in the early 1950s when she won sixteen tournaments from 1953 through 1955. She was inducted into the LPGA Hall of Fame in 1951. In all, she won fifty professional tournaments and eleven major championships (three as an amateur).

Golf has been my life for twenty-six years, so it's not easy for me to be objective about it. By and large, it's been a good life, too, so the prejudices show up more than they might with someone else. But when it comes to this fascinating and frustrating game, there are a few convictions I hold that are based on observation and are not to be classified as prejudices.

One of these convictions has to do with women and golf. There's been far too much of this nonsense, so far as I'm concerned, about women being inferior on the golf course, the people who make this claim usually basing their argument on the female's physical structure. To them I say: "If a woman can walk, she can play golf!"

I'll say also that a woman's golf game *is* different from a man's. A woman—unless she's a Patty Berg, or the late Babe Zaharias—will not be able to slam the ball down the fairway with the power that a Hogan or a Souchak brings to his game. What too many people don't realize, however, is that a women has a few natural advantages which a man doesn't have when it comes to connecting a club with its white target. One of these advantages is sensitivity—a kind of perception that gets down into her fingertips and comes out when she's holding a putter. She "feels" her game more strongly than a man.

For instance, when somebody asks me how hard I stroke a 16-foot putt, I've got to answer, "I don't know. I look at the ball; I look at the cup; I take in the kind of lie I've got. And when I've done that, I just *feel* I've got to hit the ball in a certain way." This "feeling" is the most important factor in a woman's game. Women can birdie a hole on "feel" alone.

Perhaps the first consideration for a woman golfer is the reaction she will suffer from walking into this man's world. She will feel diffident about taking up a game so long dominated by the male sex. There isn't really very much I can say about this. The only mistake I'd caution against is the natural one a woman can make under these circumstances: over-aggression. Play the game as well as you know how and think of the initial breakthrough much as you would if you were moving into a new community. It seems unfriendly—at first. There is resistance—at first. But the opposition will melt before two positive qualities:

the ability to play and the grace you would manifest in any social situation.

The most important advice I'd give any woman just starting to play is: get the fundamentals down pat! It's a bad mistake simply to pick up a club and start swinging. If you can afford them, lessons from a competent pro will be worth their weight in birdies; if money is a consideration, join a group to take lessons.

When the old question, "What is the most important part of the game?" is thrown at me, I don't have to think twice. I answer, "The grip." Without that basic, anyone's form is bound to be way off. From the grip we build to the stance and from the stance we graduate to the heart of the game itself, the swing. These are the imperatives. Without them, one can't achieve even the status of a duffer; with them, one has a game. The rest is merely refinement. I know that this sounds like heresy, but too much has been said and written—mostly by men—about the intricacies of golf, and the theories behind each movement. I suggest that these theories be tossed out the window. While it is a lucky thing for us professionals that most people seem to prefer their golf theories tricked up, it is also a fact that the game is not tricky, or even complicated. I will admit that, to a considerable extent, the movements involved are unnatural movements, but that's as far as the complexity goes. Perhaps a mental picture I've carried around for years may help you.

The golf swing itself, incorporating the fundamentals, is the focal point of the game. And of that swing, including as it does the grip and the stance, the most important feature is the position of the head. So, I think of my head as the hub on a wagon wheel, the position of my arms at the successive stages of the swing as the spokes. That's all. The clubhead will describe that perfect circle. Sometimes it will go all the way, sometimes it won't, but remove that hub (fall away from the ball, jerk the head to one side), and you've lost the smooth rhythm that brings results. To carry my mental picture to its natural conclusion, should the hub go, the wheel will fall off the axle and the wagon itself will break down completely. Now, once this basic movement has been assimilated, it's merely a question of getting the women's co-ordination to the point where the swing is a natural, rhythmic, one-piece thing. At this point, she has a working game.

Let's retrace. I said that if a woman can walk, she can play golf. I'll elaborate on that a bit. If she's serious about wanting to learn the game, it doesn't make much difference whether her age is 11, 31, or 51. Suppleness is an asset, lack of it a limitation, but a reasonably active woman who takes up the game at 51 will still be able to become a completely competent golfer. Nor will a woman's size make any appreciable difference. To some extent, size will be a factor in the length of her shots, but here again, work on co-ordination can do much to make up for lack of power. Now, I'm aware that there is a vast range and variation in individual co-ordination. There are natural-born athletes, as there are natural-born dancers. But I've seen some men and women, too, who started out with two left feet on the dance floor, and who persevered until they had developed the rhythm necessary for the intricacies of the fox trot. The same thing is true of golf.

A woman who wants to play golf has definite advantages for the development of facility beyond this "feeling" I've mentioned at the beginning. A woman is, in most cases, not only more flexible, but comes very close to being double-jointed. She may never suspect that this is so, but she'll find out in jig-time when she begins working on grip and swing. It is often much easier for her to adapt her body to the rigors of the follow-through, for instance, than it is for her more muscular and power-conscious husband.

Once the initial shyness about taking up the game has been overcome, any woman is going to be anxious to go out on the course and settle down to actual play. There are good reasons why her instructor won't allow this for a while. For one thing, it isn't fair to penalize other players, and that's exactly what it would be for a complete novice to sail back and forth down the fairway. Moreover, her ineptitude would probably send her straight back to the pro shop to turn in her clubs. It will be far better for the club member and for the golfer's own morale if she has absorbed the rudiments of the game during her lessons and worked out the worst kinks on the practice tee. Like learning to dance—or cook—golfing is not something that comes through osmosis, and I would warn any woman taking up the game not to be discouraged. However, most people, male and female, who want to learn golf are likely to be so strongly motivated that discouragement usually turns out to be a temporary thing. I feel that women, especially, must realize that becoming an able golfer takes time. It takes time, not because women are less adequate than men on the golf course, but simply because it is a process of learning and assimilation. So many women have engaged in sports so little since their school days—if indeed they were active then—that it requires training for unused muscles to become disciplined to the rigors of a golf game. But remember that fox trot.

Also remember women have a psychological advantage. A man is expected to pick up a club and break 90 before he's spent twenty hours on the course. A woman not only is not expected to be so adept, but usually she is considered a pretty helpless little thing, totally unable to introduce clubhead to ball. There are no added pressures in her learning process.

I'd like to say one final practical word about golf for women. Golf is really three games. There's the long game, where women are at a disadvantage. There's a short game, where women are at no disadvantage at all; in fact, if they've worked on their co-ordination and perception, they are ahead of that game by a mile. And then there is the game that is really eighteen games in one. Each hole is a miniature golf game, an individual challenge, an individual chance to "feel" the pitfalls of the course and attempt to beat the odds. Women are marvelous at this kind of thinking. A woman can and does think of a particular hole (say, a par five) as a small world in itself. As a matter of fact, this is where the "thinking game" comes in. Tommy Armour, one of the finest golfers and teaching pros of all time, knows this and has preached it for years. And before Tommy, there was Walter Hagen, perhaps the all-time great, who flatly refused to think about the hole he had just played or the one that was ahead of him. The only pin in the world for Hagen was the one he was shooting for at that minute. This is campaigning, and here the ladies are masters—or mistresses, if you insist. The only additional tip I can give is: Avoid self-pity at all costs. It will ruin a game faster than four bogies in quick succession!

So, it may take a year before a woman feels comfortable on the course. It will take longer before her handicap is as low as her husband's. It won't take even a year, however, before she begins to realize that while her golf game will be different from a man's, it can most certainly be just as good. What's even more important, it will be one that will give her all the self-confidence in the world, since she will come to appreciate her own deftness, sensitivity, and capacity for meeting a situation coolly, and she will learn to use her non-aggressive, but competitive, spirit. All a woman has to remember is that if she can walk, she can play golf!

No one can beat Marlene Hagge at pulling out of a seemingly impossible lie. Anyone who has ever watched Beverly Hanson hit the long irons cannot doubt her control or the power behind it. In a few particulars, these golfers will contradict each other. That's good—for golf and its players. Golf is a highly individual game. Barbara Romack, one of the really fine performers, tells us that she doesn't allow her hands to turn over in a punch shot; I do. My suggestion to the golfer is to try it both ways. The method that's most comfortable is the one that will produce results for you.

Women may not have the muscle; they do have the intelligence. And also, I think, the sense of humor that golf demands. This last is a necessity, for golf is very much like a love affair: if you don't take it seriously, it's no fun; if you do, it breaks your heart. Don't break your heart, but flirt with the possibility.

Louise Suggs's successful career was primarily due to her fine shot-making—where her routine never varied. Her beautiful smooth and rhythmic trademark swing was soundly joined together so that she gained tremendous speed through the hitting area. She was often named the Ben Hogan of women's golf. And rightfully so—not only was her swing a match to Hogan's, but her quiet, intense concentration on the course gave her a Hoganesque quality as well.

"You Don't Have the Responsibilities People Have in the Real World."

Betsy Rawls

from *Gettin' to the Dance Floor,* 1986

Betsy Rawls started playing golf at age seventeen; later than most great players. After a few amateur wins, she quickly turned professional and joined the new LPGA Tour in 1951. Within a few months she took home the United States Women's Open Championship trophy (a tournament she would continue to win three more times). Her impressive total of fifty-five tournament wins made her third in all-time rankings, and in 1952 she was the number one player in earnings. She went on to win ten LPGA tournaments in 1959, and at the relative young age thirty-two, she was the fifth member to be inducted into the LPGA Hall of Fame in 1960.

After her retirement in 1975, Betsy Rawls became active in the behind-the-scenes work of women's golf. As the LPGA's tournament director for six years, she was brilliant in dealing with sponsors—making the purses much larger than in the early days. Her work was and is one of the reasons the LPGA is so successful today.

My father was the only one in my family who played golf, and he taught me the basics. Then I started taking lessons from Harvey Penick at the Austin Country Club when I was in college at the University of Texas. For my first lesson Harvey charged me $3. Even then that wasn't a lot, but Harvey never charged a lot, so it wasn't because he knew me or anything like that. Anyway, I stayed out there with him for about an hour and a half. The next time I went out to him, when I got ready to pay he said, "No, I'm just telling you things I told you last week," and he never let me pay him again. I got a lot of mileage out of that first $3. I took lessons from Harvey for twenty years. He's the only teacher I ever had, and I owe a great deal of my success as a player to him, just as Ben Crenshaw, Tom Kite, and a lot of others do.

It didn't take me too long to become a good player, and one reason, I think, is because I started a little later than most—at seventeen. I think you can do it easier at that age than at twelve or thirteen, because you're more mature and stronger. Also, I always thought well on the course. I was a good student. Phi Beta Kappa. I studied a lot, and that helped my concentration. Maybe it helps to have a very controlled, logical sort of mind to play golf. I studied physics in college, and my father was an engineer. Maybe there's something to that. Of course, you also have to just play a lot when you're young. You have to pay those dues. When I was in college it was hard to play much, because I had a lot of math. In summer, though, I played just about every day, round and round and round.

There is always the problem of women athletes being taken as tomboys, as being too masculine. But when I started out I can't remember there being any kind of stigma attached to women athletes in Texas, at least not to women golfers. You see, golfers weren't that way, much. Most of them I ran into were at country clubs and from the upper classes, so to speak, and knew how to behave. So that didn't seem much of a problem. Eventually I was given a membership at Austin Country Club, but at the start I played golf. I played with the boys except in tournaments, carried my own bag, did a little gambling—skin games, you know—and held my own. It was fun.

Maybe we weren't socially conscious back then. Of course, women golfers are different in that they wear skirts—*we* did, anyhow—and golf is not that physical a game; you don't have to be very muscular or big. If you watched women's basketball you'd get a much different impression of women athletes. A lot of women golfers are small and feminine-looking. So we never really fought that battle. We were always conscious of needing to dress properly and look and act ladylike, and we always did.

The feminist movement never really touched the women's tour, we were all just totally unaware of it. I think that's because we were so involved in playing golf and winning tournaments. We weren't interested in furthering women's rights. We felt we had everything, and nothing to prove. We had a golden opportunity to go out there and make money if we played well. We were treated well, and had nothing to gain from the women's movement, so consequently we pretty much ignored it.

I didn't pattern my swing after anyone in particular, because for quite some time after I started I never saw a real good player, man or woman. The first good player I ever saw was Byron Nelson, in an exhibition in Fort Worth. I was absolutely amazed. I had no idea golf could be played that way, that people could hit the ball so far. I was so green. At the first tournament I entered, the Women's Texas Open, at the Colonial Country Club—imagine playing your first tournament at Colonial? Good Lord!—I didn't know anything. I didn't know people had shag bags and warmed up before they played. I came from a little town in Texas. Arlington was pretty small then, and I had never even *seen* a golf tournament before. I just went out and played, and that was it.

Anyway, I qualified for the championship flight and won my first match. But I lost my second match, to Dot Kiltie. She was runner-up once in the Women's U.S. Amateur. Then I lost in the first round of the consolation matches. I did pretty well for my first tournament ever, but I was *so* mad that I lost. I just hated losing. After that is when I really started working on it. I gathered together some practice balls and went at it. Once you play in a tournament, you get hooked on that.

I played amateur golf for only about two and a half years, because I turned pro in 1950. Wilson Sporting Goods asked me to join their staff. They had Patty Berg and Babe Zaharias, and needed someone else to do clinics and play exhibitions. I considered the offer carefully and decided that golf would be more interesting than physics. I played professional golf for almost twenty-five years, and was in on the beginnings of the Ladies Professional Golf Association. The LPGA got started in 1950, and Wilson hired Freddie Corcoran to be tournament director. Wilson needed places for Patty and Babe to play. Eventually, MacGregor and Spalding, the other two major equipment manufactures at the time, joined Wilson to help pay Freddie's salary. Fred booked tournaments, but that's all he really did; none of the promotional stunts he was known for when he ran the men's tour. We handled the day-to-day operation of our tour, did it all, and it was a kind of interesting situation. One of us kept the books and wrote out the checks, someone else did all the correspondence. I look back and can remember making rulings on other players in a tournament I was competing in. In this day and time, good gracious, you'd probably get sued for something like that.

We didn't have any staff, because we couldn't afford to hire people. That was the situation for a long time. I mean, the average purse in our tournaments was $3,000, perhaps $4000—total. Five thousand was a good tournament in the early 1950s. Can you imagine that? But, you know, it didn't seem like a small amount. It was fine for us. We were happy to get that much, and didn't mind that the men pros were getting so much more for their tournaments. You see, we didn't compare ourselves to men pros, or expect as much.

How do I account for that feeling? I guess the men are more spectacular. They hit the ball farther, score better, are just better players because of their strength. It's simply a matter of strength. I think that's the only way they differ. Then, again, we could have our moments. One year six of us women pros were in England and played the British Walker Cup team, the country's best men amateurs. We beat them, and, oh, it was a black day in England for them! We played doubles in the morning and were behind by one point, but in the afternoon singles every woman won her match. We had Babe, Patty Berg, myself, Betty Jameson, Peggy Kirk, and Betty Bush. Well, those men were just stricken. They just couldn't believe it. We played at Wentworth, the "Burma Road" course, and from the same tees as the men— about in the middle of the members' men's tees. It was the funniest thing. The press made a big thing about it.

On our circuit at home, in the early days, we drove almost everyplace. We didn't have as many tournaments as they have now, so we didn't play every week. I got my own car my second year on the tour, a Cadillac, which everyone drove because of its weight and room for clubs and baggage. We would travel two in a car, and caravan. Caravanning was following each other on the road, usually two cars. It was fun. I got to see the country. We drove across the United States at least twice a year, and did a lot sightseeing. Driving through the Rockies, we'd stop and have picnics. I know if I were starting out now I would never see the country, because I would fly everyplace. I would see the golf course, the hotel, the airport, and that's it. So today's players miss a lot, I think, by not driving. Of course, it's impractical to drive now, but I'm glad we did it.

In the beginning a women could get on the tour by just showing up. She would apply to join the LPGA and come out and play. She was either good enough to stay on tour or she wasn't. Money was the only limiting factor. If she ran out, she had to get some more or not play. People didn't turn pro back then unless they were good players, because the only appeal was golf. Nowadays there are other things that appeal to players— the life, the exposure, the endorsements, being on television. In the early days you just made out from the purse money, and the only reason you did it was because you loved to play golf.

When I first turned pro, there were only fifteen people playing our tour regularly. Then it went to about twenty, and gradually built up. Now, almost every good amateur turns pro. And back then the galleries weren't that big. But we didn't worry about that too much. We thought of the tour as more of a competition than a show. We thought of it as playing a tournament and producing a winner. The first prize would usually be around $1,000. We all decided at one of our meetings how much the winner would get, and then break down the remaining money places. There was no particular formula for that. I must have made up a hundred formulas over the years. We just figured what percentage of the total purse we wanted to give first place—it was usually fifteen percent—then go from there. It was an unwieldy process sometimes, because there were people who felt strongly about certain issues. Anytime you talked about money there would be vehement discussions. But, to everyone's credit, I can't think of any wrong decisions that were made.

We had some tournament sponsors in the first years who were kind of patrons and saw us through. The first was Alvin Handmacher, who made Weathervane suits for women. The next big one was Sears, Roebuck. But most of the tournaments were sponsored by local organizations, the Lions Club or Chamber of Commerce. They could afford to put one on because the prize money was low and it was nice for the community.

We had some sponsors who reneged on the prize money. There was one in Oklahoma City, I remember, but it wasn't Waco Turner. He had plenty of money and we never had anything to worry about with Waco. He put on two or three tournaments for us. He built his own course in Burneyville, Oklahoma, out in the wilderness. The course was so new when we played there the first time, and so badly built. I remember Bob Hagge and some other guy who was on tour with us went out to cut the cups, and the greens were so hard they couldn't get them cut. They had to hammer them out. So they didn't change the cups for the rest of the week. That was when Waco was paying so much for every birdie and eagle you made, and I remember having a good week. I won the tournament and made two or three eagles, which were worth $500 apiece. I walked away with all kinds of money.

Then there was Tam O'Shanter in Chicago, George S. May's tournament. That was the biggest event on our tour, the biggest purse we played for. It was very exciting, because you got to see everybody in the whole world, the whole golf world at least. There was a tournament for men and women pros and men and women amateurs. Four tournaments at once. It was quite a phenomenon. It's hard to find a tournament to compare with Tam O'Shanter in excitement. Everybody in the game was there, the money was terrific, the clubhouse facilities were special, and there were the biggest crowds. People came out and had picnics in the rough. First time I ever saw that. And it was fun to see all the top men pros and amateurs, and foreign players. I watched Sam Snead and Ben Hogan and other great men players. But I didn't get much of lasting value from their swings that I could use in mine.

The strength of my game was the short game. I could really scramble well, manufacture shots, and play out of difficult situations. I always got a kick out of that. Driving was my weakest part, and whenever I did drive well I won tournaments. But nobody is ever going to be better than Mickey Wright.

Mickey was much better than Babe Zaharias. No comparison. Babe was stronger, and maybe a better athlete—she was so well coordinated—but Mickey had a better golf swing, hit the ball better, could play rings around Babe. See, I think Babe got started in golf too late. She didn't really take it up until she was past thirty. If she had started as a kid, the way Mickey did, maybe nobody would ever have beaten her. She was just that good an athlete. And Babe loved to win. Or she hated to lose is the better way to put it. She was absolutely the worst loser I ever saw. She wasn't a bad sportsman, but if things didn't go her way she could show her displeasure. She didn't like it when people crossed her. I guess that's often the way with great athletes.

The sponsors made all the decisions about running their tournaments in the early days, and I must say they were greatly influenced by Babe Zaharias. And Babe was not above saying she would drop out of a tournament if this or that wasn't done. She knew how much they really needed her, and they did. She was the draw, really. For instance, back in '51 we were playing someplace and Babe was leading the tournament. Patty Berg was second. They were paired together for the last round, in the last group, and Babe started out horrendously. So Patty caught her and passed her. Then it started raining. They were near the clubhouse at the time and Babe marched in there and told the sponsors it was raining and she wanted the round canceled. And they did it. They rescheduled for the next day. It wasn't even close to being rained out, or the course being unplayable. Well, Patty was absolutely furious, just livid. But Patty beat Babe the next day anyway. Played rings around her.

But I loved Babe. She was good to play with, fun to be around. She was very witty and kept the gallery laughing all the time. Wisecracks all the way around. Very uninhibited. She was a little crude, and some things she said shocked me a little because I was just the opposite, but the gallery loved her. There will never be another like her.

Sometimes we resented Babe for the way she was in cases like the rain-out. I didn't admire her tactics then, but I never really got angry with her. She was just that way. The thing I objected to more was that we had no control over sponsors being influenced in that way, that they could do whatever they pretty much pleased. I think the sponsors treated us in such a high-handed way for two reasons: because we were women, and because we weren't that big a draw and needed them more than they needed us. They felt they were doing us a favor, and didn't look upon us as great athletes. It was just a matter of having a nice little tournament; fun having the girls come to town, I guess. I didn't have a big problem living with that sort of thing, though, mainly because there was nothing to compare it with. If we had been able to look into the future and see how tournaments would be run and what kind of control the organization would have, I'm sure we would have been appalled. But back then we didn't know any differently. We had our hand out, and couldn't be too demanding.

In those early years the local greens superintendent or pro would set the cups and tee markers, and as a result we played tough courses. We would never play a ladies' tee. It was generally from the middle or the back of the men's tees. They just couldn't stand it for the women to score well on their courses. We played some monstrous courses, much longer than they play now. And pin placements were tough. But nobody ever thought of complaining. There was nothing wrong with long courses; everybody had to play them. It was when we got so concerned with our public image and the scores in the newspapers that we became concerned with long courses. But back then it didn't matter if you shot a 75, so long as you won the tournament.

But I remember Patty Berg shooting 64 at the Richmond Country Club in California—a tough course. I was playing with her, and to this day it may be the best round of golf I've ever seen played. Now the players come close to shooting 64, but on courses that were nothing like those we played in the early years. Those courses averaged 6,400 yards. Then, again, I didn't want any shorter courses. Mickey and Babe had an advantage on them, and so did I, although Mickey would have won on any golf course, any length. Anyway, the cream really came to the top on a 6,400-yard course. You just had to have a good swing to play it, or you'd have a 90.

In the early days there was not much of a future for women pros in golf after tournament life. There were very few if any club jobs available. But I don't think the really good players ever thought that far ahead. Patty Berg, Louise Suggs, myself, we had contracts with Wilson and MacGregor and had clubs made with our names on them, so we didn't have to worry too much. But when you got past the first five, it was a problem. I don't know that any of them were prepared for living without tournament golf. When you're playing the tournament circuit you think you'll always play and there will never come a time when you will have to do something else, quit and go to work. People become addicted to it. It's a very protected kind of existence. You don't have the responsibilities people have in the real world. You go from place to place, and nowadays sponsors take care of all your needs—they meet you at airports, provide so many services. You don't have to make beds, do wash, and such mundane things. People hate to give that up, even players who aren't having a lot of success, and I'm afraid a lot of them don't prepare for life after tournament golf. I had a lot of success, and can't imagine anyone staying out there as long as I did without winning.

It was a shock for me to quit the tour. I had withdrawal symptoms. It was traumatic. But that was mainly in making the decision to quit. Once I did it, I got so involved in the work of a tournament director that it never bothered me at all.

Now it's much easier for women to get club-professional jobs. They are in great demand. More women golfers want to take lessons from women pros. I get a lot of offers to take a teaching job. Women pros are admired now. The women's movement probably has something to do with that, and being on television. Women pros are admired now.

I won fifty-five tournaments as a professional. I won ten of them in 1959, and won a little over $26,000. But I don't feel any resentment at the amount of money the girls are playing for now. That's not why I played, for the money. If it was a lot of money I was after, I probably would have done something else. I thoroughly enjoyed playing and got a lot of satisfaction out of it. I take pride in being a pioneer that helped make today's tour possible.

Although Betsy Rawls was not a long hitter, she had a terrific short game and was considered one of the best shotmakers of all time. Through sheer grittiness, she seemed to be able to get the ball into the hole from just about anywhere. The LPGA Tour players used to say of her game, "she could get it up and down from out of a garbage can."

This One's On Me

Mickey Wright
from *Play Golf the Wright Way*, 1962

Mary Kathryn (or Mickey) Wright is usually one of first players mentioned when talking about the greatest players of all time. She had a golf swing that even Ben Hogan felt was the most perfect he had ever seen. She was a magnificent player and a great favorite of her fellow professionals. Her father introduced her to the game at age seven, and by thirteen, she was consistently shooting in the 80s.

As an amateur, she won several tournaments, including the World Amateur in Chicago. In 1954, at the age of nineteen, she turned professional and went on to have a dazzling career that included four wins at the United States Women's Open Championship (1958, 1959, 1961, and 1964), plus at least one victory every year during her fourteen years on the LPGA Tour. The demands of tournament golf, however, took their toll on Mickey, and in 1969 at age thirty-four she stopped playing regularly. She had won a total of eighty-two professional tournaments.

When I was seven years old, my father bought me a toy set of golf clubs from a dime store in San Diego, my home town. I swung so hard with those little tin clubs I broke every one of them.

I still swing hard. But now I know what I'm doing.

After my first disastrous venture into golf, I didn't swing a club again until I was eleven, a blond, chunky, oversized girl,

5'9", my present height. I'm grateful now that I'm tall for I have long arms which give me a long arc and help me to hit a longer ball, but when I was eleven and big for my age, I would have given anything to be small and dainty like Johna Lou Kimball who lived down the street.

If I had been small and dainty like Johna Lou, I've wondered since, would I have taken up golf with the zest and zeal that I did?

Something happened to me when I swung a golf club. I felt free and graceful and like somebody. I still do. Golf to me is not only a way of life, it's a creative outlet, a constant, never-ending challenge; frustrating, but never dull; infuriating, but satisfying.

Golf has brought me more rewards, financially and personally, than I ever could have earned had I become the psychology teacher I set out to be when I enrolled in Leland Stanford University at Palo Alto, California, in the summer session of 1952. I never finished college or the course, for in November 1954, when I was nineteen, I became a professional golfer and the youngest member on the tour of the Ladies Professional Golf Association. I feel as if I've earned my own version of a master's degree in psychology in study and experience, trial and error on golf courses throughout the United States, for psychology, I've learned, is as integral a part of good golf as an efficient swing.

I was born on Valentine's Day, 1935, and christened Mary Kathryn after my mother, Kathryn, a beautiful Southern belle from Atlanta, Georgia. My father, Arthur F. Wright, a successful San Diego attorney and one-time president of the California State Bar Association, was fifty-two when I was born. He wanted a boy and had the name Michael picked out. When Michael turned out to be Mary Kathryn, he compromised and nicknamed me Mickey.

My parents were divorced when I was three. Each has remarried. My father, a former football player at the University of

Michigan, enjoyed sports of all kinds. He thought I could be a good athlete more as a form of self-expression than as a career. I started to walk when I was nine months old and my co-ordination always has been good. Dad bought me a baseball glove and bat when I was four, and used to get out in his backyard and pitch to me and throw the ball so hard my hands would hurt from catching it.

Unwittingly, he was contributing to my becoming a good golfer, for "ball sense" is a great asset to a woman golfer. The instinctive feeling of normal release in throwing a ball, with the same underhand, natural reflex action as pitching a horseshoe or lagging a penny finds its counterpart in golf, especially in the short game and putting where judgment of distance is the main objective.

My father liked golf. An average player with the analytical mind of an attorney, he worked constantly at understanding and improving his game. Frequently, when he went to a driving range to practice, he took me along. So at the ripe age of eleven, I, too, had my cubicle on the practice tee, a bucket of balls, and a borrowed club. Hour after hour, I stood swinging away with all my might. All I wanted to do was hit, hit, hit, the more the merrier.

Finally, brimming over with enthusiasm and self-confidence, characteristics uncharacteristic of me at the age of eleven, I pestered my father to let me play golf with him at the La Jolla Country Club, about 18 miles from San Diego. This was more than he had bargained for so he did what any good lawyer would do. He asked for a postponement.

"Take some lessons first and *then* I'll play golf with you," he promised.

And so I met Johnny Bellante, the golf professional at the La Jolla Country Club (and now the pro at the Chapultepec

Country Club in Mexico City). Johnny was about forty, hand-
some, dark-haired, a fine teacher and a beautiful swinger of the
golf club. He had unlimited patience, besides, which he needed
with me.

I'll never forget that first lesson. Like an overwhelming
Newfoundland puppy, not quite housebroken but willing to
make up in floppy affection what I lacked in behavior, I showed
up on the practice tee, wearing sneakers and pedal pushers and
an "I'll-show-you-how-far-I-can-hit-the-ball" expression.

Johnny had trained puppies before; a soothing voice, a kind
word, but you must obey the master's commands. I obeyed.
There is no better time to learn golf than when you are young
and anxious and willing and uncomplicated. You don't question
anything the teacher tells you. You just do it like a little monkey.
Your body is agile and limber. Your muscles respond. Your im-
mature mind doesn't dominate the swing.

From the very beginning, Johnny tried to teach me the feeling of a free, rhythmic, gradually accelerating swing; to reach
the maximum speed or momentum at contact, another secret of
hitting the ball long.

Johnny made a switch from a eucalyptus tree branch, handed
it to me and said, "Mickey, I want you to swing this until you
can make it sing."

To make that switch sing, I had to move it as correctly as I
would a golf club. I discovered that it reached its highest pitch
at the bottom point of the swing. If I tried to make it sing by
swinging it from on top, by forcibly assisting it with my body,
my arms, my hands, my shoulders, it wouldn't sing. It wouldn't
even groan. It just wasted its momentum and wound up limp,
spent, and ineffective.

To make that switch sing, I literally had to let it have its head
to reach its own normal momentum and to delay the blow until

the switch had returned to its original address position, then it would truly sing.

I took lessons from Johnny Bellante for three years. He was also Gene Littler's first teacher, and it must have given Johnny great satisfaction in 1961 when two of his protégés from the same town, Gene Littler and Mary Kathryn Wright, won the Men and Women's United States Opens. I know it did me. I had won it twice before, in 1958 and 1959, but each time I win the Open—and I hope I win it many more times—there is the secret satisfaction of a little girl with a most cherished possession.

Johnny also worked on balance and rhythm with me, two "musts" in any good golf swing. No matter how they swing, all good golfers have one thing in common, balance and rhythm.

To teach me balance, Johnny had me stand on one foot and swing, then he had me stand with my feet close together and swing.

If you can swing from either of these positions without toppling over, then you have an inkling of what a balanced swing should feel like.

By summer's end, I got so I could pretty regularly hit a ball 175 or 200 yards. Johnny was so pleased with his pupil he telephoned the San Diego *Union* and asked the newspaper to send out a photographer. The *Union* not only printed my picture but captioned it questionably, "The Next Babe?"

What I liked best about the picture was the fact that my schoolmate at Woodrow Wilson Junior High saw it and looked at me, I thought, with a tinge of admiration and respect. That was my first taste of recognition. I savor it still.

There are times when I think I always had a good swing, but I have home movies of my first six months of learning which tell me differently and help to keep me humble. In them, I look like the worst woodchopper imaginable with a typical beginner's swing; a bad grip, a closed clubface going away from the ball and a flying right elbow which pointed away from the ground at the top of the swing. At the start of the downswing I worked the club to the outside and cut across the ball, a perfect slice or push position.

Apart from my schoolwork and activities, golf became my all-encompassing passing passion. Slowly I lost interest in Tommy Goodbody, my childhood beau and dancing partner. Every chance I had, I'd play golf or take a lesson or practice by myself. La Jolla Country Club is full of canyons and I managed to visit five or six of them in each round of golf. Inevitably I had three or four unplayable lies. I was long and I was wild and I loved every minute of it. It usually took me two or three shots to get out of a sand trap, I three-putted practically every green. Slowly but surely, things began to fall into place.

At the end of the first year, I broke 100, still one of my greatest golfing thrills. The second year I broke 90, and the fourth year, when I was fifteen, I shot a 70 at the Mission Valley Country Club in San Diego in a local city tournament. I remember playing with Millie Rebstock, the city and county champion at the time. That day everything went together.

After three years of working with Johnny Bellante, I studied a year with Fred Sherman, then pro at the Mission Valley Country Club, coincidentally now the site of the Mickey Wright Open, a new annual event on the LPGA Tour.

An ardent pupil, I put my teachers on a pedestal, and tried my best to do anything they told me to do. I practiced faithfully, out of desire, not coercion.

In 1949, I played in the Southern California Junior Girls Tournament at the San Gabriel Country Club. I won it and won as well the discerning professional interest of Harry Pressler, the club pro.

"If you ever feel you need further help in your golf swing, I'll be happy to help you," he told me.

Before too long, with my mother's permission, I telephoned Mr. Pressler. "This is Mickey Wright. Do you remember me? I can use your help."

Are you going to be home tonight?" he asked. That very evening Harry Pressler drove all the way from Los Angeles to San Diego, had dinner with us and spent four hours giving me a lesson in the living room.

We had a big mirror there, and Harry worked on my position at the top of the swing. In that and the many lessons that followed, for which he never charged me, Harry indoctrinated me with the principle of keeping the clubface square throughout the swing; at address position; halfway through the finish of the swing.

This is the theory I subscribe to today. To achieve and maintain this square position throughout, Harry also emphasized the need and logic of rolling the weight across my feet from the left foot to the inside of the right. That was then and still is foreign to many golfers, but to me it is the mainspring of my swing.

A day or so after my living-room lesson with Harry Pressler, I played in the Indio (California) Invitational Tournament and won it with rounds of 70 and 71. For two years thereafter, every Saturday morning my mother drove me the 125 miles to Los Angeles so I could take a lesson from Harry.

Hour after hour we worked on the key points of the swing. Harry actually placed me in those "square" positions so I could learn the feel.

I practiced it so thoroughly and painstakingly that to me now *a swing is a conscious feeling of the weight and position of the clubhead at all times throughout the swing.*

Yet with all the fine teaching I had as a young girl, it took me almost six years on the LPGA Tour to learn *how to play golf;* to realize that a beautiful swing isn't enough; that strategy at times can be more effective than the swing.

In 1952 when I was seventeen, and a first-term summer student at Stanford, I won the United States Golf Association's Junior Girls' Championship at the Monterey Peninsula Country Club. Barbara McIntire, also seventeen, and National Amateur Champion of 1959, was runner up. Anne Quast (Decker), then fourteen, who started to play golf when she was three years old, and I were co-medalists with 76. Both Anne and Barbara are outstanding amateurs still. Anne, now married to a Tacoma dentist, has made her own golf history, winning the National Amateur crown in 1958 and 1961.

My winning the National Juniors and the resultant acclaim got me all fired up about golf. Psychology student or not, I was determined to make golf my career.

I started to wear glasses in 1953. I am nearsighted. At first they were hard to get used to on the golf course but they never bother me now. When it rains they can be slightly distracting for I have to stop to wipe them before every shot. (That also gives me a little time to think.) I don't like to wear a hat when I play, but I do wear a visor when it rains. I feel more secure with glasses on than without them; perhaps it's the knowledge that if I need to, with my nearsightedness, I can actually see what I have taught myself to feel in my golf swing. I tried contact lenses for a time but quickly discarded them. In the photographs illustrating my swing, I didn't wear glasses because photographer Robert Riger was fearful the sun would reflect in them and spoil a good picture.

My banner year as an amateur was 1954. I talked my father into letting me take a year off from school and financing me for a winter season on the women's tour in Florida and the South-east. I headed cross-country in my own secondhand car, an asset as essential to a touring golfer as the golf equipment itself. I average 25,000 miles a year now on my speedometer, but I've never objected to it. It's all part of the game.

In 1954 St. Petersburg Open, I lead the field of amateurs and pros with an opening day round of 68; the first time I ever broke 70. This brief taste of glory was a little too rich for my swing, and I scored 78-82 in the final two rounds, but I still finished low amateur for the tournament. I made a good showing in other tournaments which indicated to me I could play well enough to compete with the pros, so I returned to San Diego in March of 1954 and again persuaded my father to finance me for a few big tournaments that summer.

In the Amateur Division, I won the Tam O'Shanter All American and the World Championship in Chicago; was runner-up to Barbara Romack in the National Amateur; low amateur in the National Open, finishing fourth among the field with rounds of 74-79-79-76. I played the final round with the late great Babe Didrikson Zaharias who, with a total of 291, won the Open that year for the third time (1948, 1950, 1954), fifteen months after her first cancer operation.

I turned professional that fall. My first year as a professional on the tour, 1955, marked the most frustrating phase of my golfing career, ego-wise, not economically. I won $6325.18 in prize money and finished twelfth among the lady pros for the year, but I didn't win a tournament.

I thought I had a good golf swing and people told me I had. I thought I hit the ball well, yet I'd go out and not score so well as I felt I should. I probably had as poor emotional control as any of the girls on the tour right now who aren't winning tournaments. I started tampering with my swing, which is the most costly error a golfer can make during competition. No matter how you swing, in a tournament you've got to believe your swing is the right and only one for you, otherwise your confidence is destroyed and that's fatal to a golfer.

From 1955 to 1958 I went through a completely experimental period with my swing. I took lessons from Les Bolstad, a fine teacher at the University of Minnesota who works wonders with women; from Stan Kertes at the Bryn Mawr Country Club in Chicago (he was the Babe's first teacher in Los Angeles in 1933); from Harvey Penick at the Austin Country Club in Austin, Texas.

Each year I improved money-wise, but I still wasn't satisfied. Money has never been my goal in golf. Winning is.

In 1956, my second year on the tour, I won my first tournament, the Jacksonville Open, and $8253.66 for the year. In 1957, I won three tournaments, $11,131; scored a 75.38 average and was voted the Most Improved Player on the tour.

Still, I wasn't satisfied. I felt sorry for myself. I wanted to be better. I was wallowing in self-pity in 1958 after the St. Petersburg Open. I had finished out of the money and Betsy Rawls, my best friend on the tour, won the tournament. That only exaggerated in my mind my bad playing.

There is nothing more desolate than feeling sorry for yourself away from home, in a strange motel room with no one around to offer consolation or excuses for you.

"If you quit feeling sorry for yourself," said Betsy, a Phi Beta Kappa in physics and the most logical, levelheaded person I know, "you'd do better. You hit every golf shot yourself during this tournament. No one else hit any of them for you so accept the responsibility for every shot you hit."

That was the most valuable golfing advice ever given to me.

I went on to win five tournaments that year including the U.S. Open and the LPGA, the first time anyone had won them both the same year. There wasn't a single shot I didn't say to myself, "This is your own responsibility. Do as well as you can, but make no excuses for yourself."

I know of no better Golden Rule for a golfer.

That year, I went to Harvey Penick who has been Betsy Rawls' teacher since she was seventeen and a student at the University of Texas in Austin. Betsy's own record in golf, the only four-time winner of the U.S. Open (1951, 1953, 1957, 1960) and winner of ten LPGA tournaments in 1957 is fantastic because unlike most champions she didn't take up golf until she was seventeen. It helps to get an early start in golf if you want to earn a living at it.

For two weeks, I took lessons from Harvey. At the time I thought he was the most frustrating teacher I ever went to for he never once mentioned anything wrong with my swing although I had gone to him because I thought I was hitting the ball badly. Maybe I expected him to be a miracle worker, but he didn't suggest one single change in my swing. A passive, patient professional, he quietly singled out good points in my swing and told me to concentrate on them solely as a means of getting the ball around the golf course.

That went in one ear and out the other. I left Harvey feeling hostile and cheated as if I had gotten absolutely nothing from those two weeks for which he didn't charge me, but I felt I had invested my time and energy. It took nearly two years before it finally dawned on me what Harvey Penick was trying to tell me.

The most important thing is to get the ball into the hole to the best of your ability.

It used to bother me terribly that I could hit two beautiful shots to a green and two putt for a regulation par, whereas my playing partner could drive to the left rough, send her second shot to the right rough and skull an iron onto the green ten feet from the pin, then sink it for her par.

Demoralizing? Yes. But not anymore. Now, no matter how I get there, I'm happy to be there. I try to get there in the most nearly perfect way, but if I don't, I don't chastise myself, nor lose any time or concentration in self-recrimination.

My golf swing is no different now from what it was five years ago; however, since 1958, I've played many, many rounds of golf with Earl Stewart, Jr., the thirty-nine-year-old professional at the Oak Cliff Country Club in Dallas, Texas. In September 1961, Earl won the Dallas Open on his home course, the only club pro ever to win a PGA tournament under those circumstances. He shot a 67-72-68-75 to beat Doug Sanders, Gay Brewer, Jr., and Arnold Palmer, all who tied for second, one stroke behind.

Earl taught me how to play a round of golf so that every shot means something. All I demand of myself now is that the ball stays in play. I don't want to be out of bounds or in an unplayable lie or in an impossible bunker or some ghastly spot in the rough or in the woods or behind a rock or under a tree.

I wanted to be able to swing at the next shot.

When I stand up to a shot now, I ask myself: Where is the ideal place for me to hit this shot?

I look for it and at it. Then I look around it.

Then I ask myself: Where is the worst place I could hit this shot?

If my ideal spot is not too near the worst spot, allowing for the human element of margin for error, then I try to hit the ball to the ideal spot. But if trouble looms in the immediate area of the ideal spot, then I aim at the happy medium; an untroubled area where I still can swing for my par or whatever is the cheapest way, strokewise, out of the situation.

The best thing to do after a bad shot is not flail away again in anger and annoyance, but stop a moment, take a deep breath, then start swinging with conscious emphasis on maintaining balance and rhythm.

It's that "I'm going to get you out of here, ball, if it takes me all day" attitude that send scores skyrocketing. Every golfer must get a definite mental positive picture of the shot to be played and then develop that picture through the muscles.

I'm always looking for the positive picture in golf, not the negative. When I play my best golf, I feel as if I'm in a fog. Every good golfer feels this in different ways. Some feel "zeroed" in. They're not part of this world. They're standing back watching the earth in orbit with a golf club in their hands.

I think all winning golfers get themselves in a state of self-hypnosis while they play through positive concentration. The morning of a tournament I get a shaky feeling inside, perhaps "keyed up" is the better word. The days I play well are when I'm keyed up, at the right level, not too much or too little.

I overheard an amateur once ask Louise Suggs, "How long do you have to play before you get over this nervousness?"

"You never do," Louise admitted.

This is a healthy nervousness for it alerts our muscles and our mind that every shot in golf is something unto itself and should be so considered.

The more I play, the more I respect the game of golf and its constant, never-ending challenge to me as a golfer and a person.

For pure, explosive power Mickey's swing was the best. Ben Hogan described her swing as, "the finest I ever saw, man or women." Her graceful nature instinctively allowed the club to swing, smoothly, rhythmically, and beautifully. It looked the same every time and was the envy of every player who saw her.

Beginnings and On the Road with the LPGA

Kathy Whitworth, with Rhonda Glenn
from *Golf for Women*, 1990

Kathy Whitworth is one of the best players of the 1960s and 70s. She was also one of the strongest competitors, with a record eighty-eight tour wins (including five majors), breaking Sam Snead's record of eighty-four. Her golfing career spans more than twenty years, beginning when she won the New Mexico Amateur twice. She worked with the legendary teaching pro, Harvey Penick, often driving 450 miles just to take a lesson, and she attributes much of her success to his guidance.

She joined the tour in December 1958 at the age of nineteen, when Mickey Wright was the leading women player. Tall and slim, Kathy was the new kid on the block. Her essay below describes her beginning days of golf and what life was like in on the road with the LPGA. She was inducted into the LPGA Hall of Fame in 1975.

Beginnings

I was fifteen when I played my first round of golf. I was so terrible that I played by myself for an entire year before I became brave enough to play with anyone else.

We lived in Jal, New Mexico, a little community that had sprung up in the cattle country near the western border of Texas.

Since my folks weren't members of the country club, I paid green fees. Like many golf courses in that part of the West, Jal Country Club was first built with sand greens. By the time I started to play, in about 1955, we had cottonseed greens, and a short time later the greens were converted to bent grass.

Junior players were only allowed to play on weekends. During the week, I gather up a few golf balls and hit practice shots in a cow pasture.

I practiced and played for about a year before Mother and Dad decided golf wasn't a passing fancy. They joined the country club so that I could play all the time, and I began to play with my aunt and uncle, Nell and George Addison. George was a wonderful athlete, a scratch golfer with a beautiful touch around the greens, and he won almost everything in our area. Nell was a good player, too, and won the club championship and a lot of local tournaments.

My father, Morris Whitworth, played basketball in school, but I don't think he was a serious player and I never really thought of Dad as an athlete.

My mother, Dama Robinson Whitworth was athletic. She was terribly competitive and still is, for that matter. She played high school basketball. Mother's team used to travel from one little town to another, playing against local teams, and I'm sure she was a pretty good player.

I was born September 27, 1939, in Monahans, Texas, where Dad was working for a lumber company. I was the youngest of three daughters. Carlynne was the eldest, then Evelynne, then me. Shortly after I was born, we moved back to Jal and I lived there until I went on the LPGA Tour in 1959.

My mother's family homesteaded that part of the country.

Her father opened a grocery store in Jal, and they did some farming. They had cows and pigs, and I remember playing in the barn when I was growing up. My sisters and I used to try to ride calves and horses. We watched my grandfather butcher a hog, and we'd swim in the big tanks where they watered the livestock in the pasture.

Local lore says that Jal was named for the J-A-L ranch brand. It eventually became an oil and gas town, and the story was that all pipelines led to Jal. Because of our refineries, almost all of the natural gas in the Southwest came through Jal, so we had a prosperous little town, in that respect. Jal never got very big and at its peak had about 5,000 residents.

My father's father, "Whit," opened a lumber company in town and Dad worked for him for a while and, later, for several gas companies. My grandmother, Jessie Whitworth, bought a hardware store. Mother worked in the store and Dad kept Jessie's books at night, as he did for several businesses around town.

My folks were productive working people, and very active in the community. Mother had a big family, eight brothers and sisters. At one time, my cousins and aunts and uncles made up about half the population of Jal. You could hardly talk to us about anybody in town—they were probably our relatives.

Mother and Dad eventually bought Whitworth Hardware, which they ran for years. Dad was very involved in local politics. He was on the city council for years and was elected Mayor three times.

Dad has written a humor column for *The Jal Record,* our weekly newspaper, for many years. Mother is very active in the church, in community and charity organizations, and in Democratic politics.

I played all sports as I was growing up, but mostly in sandlot games. I hated physical education because we never really got to do anything but run around the basketball court, which didn't appeal to me at all, so I joined the band. I played the bass drum. My sister Carlynne was a drummer and she was sort of my idol; anything she did, I had to do. I don't know whether I could have played another instrument. I was always the biggest girl in school so I could carry the drum.

I was on the Jal High School tennis team and I was fairly proficient at tennis, depending upon the competition. In fact, that's how I started playing golf. Some of my tennis friends insisted one day that we play golf. I used my grandfather's clubs. Whit had been a pretty good golfer who shot in the 80s.

I'll never forget that first round. I was *terrible,* but that made golf a real challenge. Because other sports had come to me so naturally, I was fascinated with this game I couldn't master. Golf also appealed to me because I didn't have to rely on another person in order to play. It was just me against the golf course, and I played against myself. How well I played didn't depend on anyone else because I had par to shoot at.

In those days, the Jal Women's Golf Association traveled to quite a few little tournaments, and the members were nice enough to take me with them. My family wasn't poor, but with two other children there wasn't a lot of extra money lying around for golf. I paid my own expenses, and the members of the women's golf association saw to it that I went to tournaments by letting me ride with them. I'm sure I wasn't as grateful then as I am now. As the years go by, I look back and think about how great it was that I had nice people like that in my life.

After playing for about a year, I took lessons from Dode Forrester at Hobbs Country Club, and forty miles from home. He taught me things that I use today, including a strong hip move on the downswing.

My first real mentor was Hardy Loudermilk, our pro at Jal

Country Club. Hardy taught me a lot, then did something that showed unusual generosity and humility and caused me to take what was probably the most important step of my career. When I was seventeen, Hardy said, "I don't know enough to take you where you need to be."

Hardy had met Harvey Penick, the golf professional in Austin, Texas, who was one of the world's best and most respected teachers. Hardy said that I had advanced to a point where I needed more instruction if I was going to be a really good player, so he called Harvey and set up an appointment for me.

Mother and I drove the 450 miles to Austin and, on this trip, I spent four days taking lessons from Harvey. I hit practice balls from sunup to sundown. Harvey would keep an eye on me, even while he was giving someone else a lesson, and Mother sat behind me on the practice tee taking notes. At night, we would go to a driving range and I would practice until the lights were turned off. Harvey would also telephone Hardy back in Jal, tell him what I was working on, and when I returned home, Hardy would watch me to make sure I followed Harvey's instruction. Most of what I know about the golf swing, I learned from Harvey Penick.

In 1957, I won the New Mexico State Women's Championship in Farmington, New Mexico. The tournament had planned to present a beautiful turquoise necklace to the winner. Typically, like a seventeen-year-old, I wanted a trophy. The committee kept the necklace and sent a trophy to me, which I thought was just outstanding. Of course, today I wish I had taken the necklace!

On the Road with LPGA

In 1958, I won the state championship again and began to meet some of the women golf professionals.

Wilson Sporting Goods often sent Betsy Rawls and Mickey Wright to small towns to play exhibitions. This was thirty years ago. A young player who showed promise was big stuff back then, especially in our part of the West, so I was invited to play in these exhibitions. In our general neighborhoods, from Amarillo to Pecos, it was nothing to jump in the car and drive 400 miles to play golf, especially if you could play with the real stars of the game.

In Hobbs, New Mexico, I played with Betsy. I played with Mickey in Hobbs and then in Pecos. It became like a regular tour. Every time Mickey came to that area, there I'd be.

After we played an exhibition in Amarillo, I asked Mickey if I could talk to her. We went into the pro's office and I told her I was very seriously thinking of turning pro. Mickey thought, however, that at nineteen, I was still too young for the tour. She advised me to wait a year and to continue to work with Harvey on my swing. I followed her advice. If Mickey said it, that was the way to go.

However, I had financial backers if and when I turned pro, which was unusual for that day. Dad, Hardy, George Blocker, who owned a gas company, and George Kendrick, who worked for El Paso Natural Gas, had agreed to put up $5,000 a year for three years. The only stipulation was that I was to give them 50 percent of my winnings during that time, which turned out to be nothing. When we discussed my career at home, Mother and Dad said, "Well, let's just do it." I agreed. And that was it.

I sent my application to the LPGA in January, 1959. Mother and I hit the highways in my little green Plymouth. My first professional tournament was the Mayfair Open in Sanford, Florida. We believed all the propaganda about how warm Florida was in the winter and almost froze to death. It was so cold that Mother and I would hurry back to the motel after I

played, jump into our beds, and pull the covers over our heads
to get warm.

Two other players turned pro that year: Mary Ann Reynolds
and Barbara Romack. Their amateur records were much better
than mine. Barbara, a former U.S. Women's Amateur champion,
was a great player, and Mary Ann had won some big tournaments. You band together when you're the new kids on tour, so
Mary Ann and I became friends and that helped me because I
was quite shy. Eventually I got to know some of the other girls
and some of the nice people in our tournament towns.

Those were great times. Our purses were meager by today's
standards, but you could make a living, and the top players made
a very good living. Of necessity, because we were always on the
road and there were only a few dozen players, we were closer,
too. After a tournament, we'd always sit around together and
have a party. Usually the winner would buy the drinks because
she was the only one who had any money!

We ran all the tournaments ourselves. We had a pairings
committee, a rules committee, and a course set-up committee.
We even did our own publicity. In fact, all of us were very pub-
lic-relations conscious. We really believed in the association and
its potential, but we felt that the only way we could really sell
it was to capture the good will of our galleries and sponsors.
We worked hard to be friendly, cooperated with the press, and
attended all of the Pro-Am cocktail parties. It worked. We got
a lot of grass roots support from golf fans, and we were able to
keep our tour going. I believe very firmly that this approach still
works, and I try to foster that sort of spirit today.

We went to great lengths to keep up our public image. We
knew we had to look sharp, neat, and well-ironed, with our
shoes polished. We even had fines for temperamental outbursts.
If you threw a club, you'd get tabbed for $50. One of our players,

JoAnne Prentice, better known as Fry, had a terrible temper. We had a rule that if you tossed a club, it couldn't touch the ground or you'd be fined. One day Fry missed an iron shot and heaved a club into the air. Just about the time the club reached the peak of its arc, Fry remembered the $50 fine, frantically circled under the falling club, and made a diving catch worthy of Willie Mays.

In off-hours, we often split into two groups, the bridge players and the poker players. I wasn't real good at either, but it was a nice way to pass the time between tournament rounds. Betty Jameson, the Hall-of-Famer and former U.S. Open champion, was a fanatical hearts player. She even wore a green eyeshade when she played. She may have worn the eyeshade because she had great peripheral vision. For that reason, it was difficult to play golf with Betty. She could see so many things going on around her that she was easily distracted by other players. I have great peripheral vision, too. I can see a lot of movement to the side even when I'm looking straight ahead, and it can be very distracting. Betty had a reputation for moving her playing partners around. She'd be standing over a putt, head anchored, eyes straight at the ball, and without moving, she'd gesture frantically for some player thirty yards away to move! For that reason, tournament golf, with its galleries and other distractions, was difficult for her.

Years later, Betty remarked, "Too bad I never played with you."

"Yes, you did," I said. "I just stayed in the trees on every hole so I wouldn't bother you."

Betty had a very solid swing, very compact. She was built very solidly and looked like she was going to hit the ball well when she stood up to it. Good grip, good address position. The only thing that hurt her was her timing, which would sometimes get a little fast. But I enjoyed watching her play.

Mary Lena Faulk was another of our good players. Mary

Lena hit a little draw and that ball just ran like a little bunny. She was a great fairway wood player and had a really impressive short game, better than that of most players. She's a wonderful lady and never had a bad word to say about anybody. Under the most trying circumstances, she'd find something good in everything. You could depend on Mary Lena.

I loved watching these great women golfers play and learned a lot by studying them carefully, particularly Patty Berg, Mickey Wright, Betsy Rawls, and Louise Suggs.

I'd watch Suggs and wonder, "How is she so consistent? Why is she always able to hit her shots the same way? Why does she have the same routine while putting, chipping, and hitting full shots?"

Louise's routine never varied. All good players have that routine because it helps build your confidence. Timing and feel change from day to day and, if you go through the same routine, you have a better chance of hitting the ball the same way each time.

I have a great deal of respect for Louise. Her execution was so great, she was like a machine. She wasn't a flashy player or one who comes crashing out of the trees all the time. She executed her shots so well that she was seldom in trouble. Louise and I have sort of the same temperament; we don't talk a lot on the golf course, so she was very pleasant to play with.

Betsy Rawls was another player I've always admired. Her record speaks for itself. She's a four-time U.S. Women's Open Champion, a member of the LPGA Hall of Fame, and today remains a key administrator in women's golf.

As a player, Betsy had a good swing but she had one of the best short games I've ever seen. She had a very soft touch around the green and a wonderful approach to putting. Long ago, I read of her putting philosophy in a magazine article and

I've followed it since. Betsy always tried to putt the ball to the hole, rather than stroking a putt past the hole, because she felt that such a stroke helped her take advantage of all the corners.

Betsy has a terrific mind. She was Phi Beta Kappa at the University of Texas, and a great thinker on the golf course. Although I never talked to her about her course strategy, I assume that she played the percentages. She never gave up. You never knew if she was shooting 60 to 90 because she was trying so hard on every shot. I believe her great reasoning ability helped her develop that attitude.

Another thing that made Betsy a great player was her ability to be unemotional on the golf course. I hardly ever saw her show any temper or any elation, which is good because it's hard to play well when you're going through a lot of highs and lows.

Her short game was exceptional. She could get the ball up and down from almost anywhere. I'll never forget seeing her get it up and down from the side of a mountain. We were playing Esmerelda Golf Course in Spokane, Washington. On a short par 4 dogleg right around a mountain, Betsy cut the corner a bit too close on her drive and the ball bounded up the side of the hill. We weren't even sure we could find the ball. When we did find it, Betsy analyzed the situation and proceeded to create some type of shot, managed to hit the ball close to the green, then chipped it close to the hole and made her putt for a par. There was no quit. As long as she saw some way, she'd do it. You could just see her mind clicking away.

That was early in my career and it made a big impression on me.

When Betsy retired, she became the LPGA's first tournament director. She was extremely good at it—good with people and good at making policies and judgments. She would never allow her personal feelings to interfere with her decisions as to what was fair and right.

I have a great deal of respect and admiration for Betsy and today consider her a good friend. I feel very close to her, in the sense that I shared her career with her and watched her put her imprint on LPGA policies that we still use today.

What I most admire about these women—Betsy, Louise, and others—is that, had it not been for their desire to play, we would not have a tour today. They started from zero. Of course, they had a lot of help, from the sporting goods companies, for example. That brings me to Patty Berg. Patty worked for Wilson Sporting Goods before a women's pro tour existed. Patty got Wilson's support for the tour through her personal dedication, the respect that the Wilson people had for her playing ability, and their personal fondness for her. For these women to start from scratch in 1950 and establish a tour that is still going today, and doing quite well, is a marvelous thing. I can't think of many of us who would have that much gumption and fortitude today.

So, at nineteen, I was a rookie on the LPGA Tour, and thrilled to be there. I was a pro! I hadn't signed with an equipment company, but Wilson was giving golf equipment to me. I had a big new golf bag and a shag bag of practice balls. My game, however, didn't match my enthusiasm and, as the season progressed, I became very discouraged. I almost quit during my first year. I was playing terribly and not making any money, so I drove home to discuss the future with Mother and Dad. They convinced me to give it a little more time, to keep trying. I returned to the tour feeling a little better about my career. The next week, in Asheville, North Carolina, I tied with two other players for the last prize check. We split $100. I had won $33. I called home, feeling as good as if I'd won the tournament.

As the quiet player on tour, Kathy Whitworth excelled in her ability to concentrate on each shot. She believed that thinking about anything else—winning a tournament or losing a tournament—was a complete waste of time and a distraction. According to her, success on the golf course is achieved by putting together a string of well-executed individual shots. If you do that well, you will end up winning. The really important thing is to do the best you can with each situation you find yourself in.

III

Modern Day Players

Women's Golf Comes of Age

"I think it's both thrilling and wonderful to be female,
both in being a women and in being a women golfer."
Nancy Lopez

My Game of Golf

Judy Rankin
from *A Natural Way to Golf,* 1976

Although Judy Rankin began playing golf at an early age—six years old—she was a late bloomer on the LPGA Tour, going winless from 1962, when she first joined the tour, until 1968 when she finally broke through and won the Corpus Christi Open. After that, she became a consistent winner on tour, accumulating twenty seven victories in the next eleven years, including the 1976 Colgate-Dinah Shore Winner's Circle and the 1977 Peter Jackson Classic, both now designated "majors" on the LPGA Tour. She won the Vare Trophy three times in 1973, 1976, and 1977, and was LPGA Player of the Year in 1976 and 1977. Due to chronic back problems, she retired from the tour in 1983. In 1996 and 1998, she was selected to be the United States captain of the LPGA's Solheim Cup team. She led the United States to victory in both matches, and she remains active today as one of the best commentators for televised golf.

My game of golf developed more or less through trial and error. Throughout my life, my father has been my number-one teacher. He is a weekend player, and his strongest point as a golfer is his love for the game. After a lot of plotting on my part, he let me try hitting balls and from then on we learned the game together. Actually, as a teacher he learned the game better than I, but now, some twenty years later, I believe I understand what we were striving for then. I was only six years old, and when you think of it, a beginning golfer has no more knowledge of the golf swing than a six-year-old. So, if everything is put in very simple, basic terms—exactly the way it was put to me—the beginner has a better chance of understanding. Now understanding something and being able to do it are two different things, but I have learned that those players with a sound knowledge of the game have a substantial advantage when it comes to maintaining a golf swing. One thing that I've noticed in good players is an ability to abide by the simple mechanical thoughts that they have used throughout their careers. When a good golfer gets to playing poorly, he or she is not striving to learn something new about the golf swing. No one, myself included, will try to find a new system or a little gimmick to straighten out his game. You simply try to return to the good, simple fundamentals that are easy and that work so well. A number of younger players on tour, along with most weekend amateurs, have not learned the beauty of a basic approach to the game of golf. Every day they turn to a new system, always thinking that they're not hitting the ball because some magical move is missing. When you begin doing this, nothing about your swing becomes familiar and all of a sudden you're absolutely lost.

I always keep notes of my key thoughts. My father has kept some notes for me at various times when I have come to him in the midst of a slump. And we've always managed to find the mistakes that were creeping into my action and causing me to play poorly. I keep track of those little mistakes. I also try to make notes at times when I am hitting the ball very well. You would be surprised at some of the very basic things that I go back to twenty-four years later for help. The Triple Crown, in January 1975, was a good example. I really had to work hard during a short span of time to prepare myself for the tournament. The weather in Midland, Texas, was not that good and I worked as much as I could in the cold weather, but when I got to Florida I was by no means ready. I finally reached a point where I was hitting the ball well, but even so I found that every sixth or seventh shot I would lose everything and hit the ball miles off to the right. Now there's no way that you can hope to play tournament golf if you hit one out of every six shots off into never-never land. I was getting pretty frantic about the whole thing, and I dreaded the thought of things going like that once the tournament began. It appeared as though this periodic wildness was simply the result of some bad timing, since I was striking the majority of my shots fairly well. So I went back to one of the most basic things that I ever learned about golf—moving everything away from the ball in one piece. I find that this thought creates a good starting base from which to establish some sort of workable timing pattern. I went back to this simple key and managed to play through the entire tournament without hitting any bad shots to the right.

When I began learning the game, my father would take me out to a driving range and make certain that the fundamental elements were correct. Though I have a very strong grip right now, I started out with an orthodox grip and a fundamentally sound address posture. I would take a wood and stand on the tee and make about a third of a swing, a few feet back and then through. I just sort of bopped the ball out off the end of the tee, and I did that until I had the basic motion mastered, until my father thought that it was correct. As I progressed I would take it back a bit farther each time, and pretty soon we had built a golf swing. I didn't begin simply by swinging at the ball and then making all sorts of adjustments and corrections. We built the swing from the bottom up, from its simplest form into a full, useable action. So the basic swing that I learned never had very many mistakes in it; we never let it get so far off track that a real flaw would develop. Things were done right the first time. After assembling a basic swing, all that was left for me to develop was a method of playing the various shots needed to score well.

I suppose there are different routes that one can travel when putting together a golf game. I can assume that I have some sort of natural ability—I have a certain talent for golf, but I am not an all-round athlete. I am athletic where golf is concerned, but I don't do other things very well. My golfing talent allows me to change things and make adjustments more readily than the average player. Someone may tell me to do something and immediately I will be able to do it without having them explain in detail or demonstrate. So there must be a type of natural feel for the swing at work within my physical makeup. Yet I have seen good players who have almost no natural feel for the game. They have succeeded in manufacturing a mechanical swing through sheer determination and hard work. There are other people who never manage to build a top golf game, even though they appear to have a good deal of inborn ability. In all facets of life there are people who have to work harder than others to achieve a certain goal. It is one of those things that just happen to be.

The person with natural talent has a bit of an advantage in starting out if he or she is able to combine ability with hard work. I don't think that you can bank on getting by solely on ability, although there are those who at times can succeed purely on the basis of some tremendous natural feel. But those players who get to the top and stay there are testimony to the value of determined effort. Kathy Whitworth is an example of a player who has relied to a large extent upon feel and natural sensitivity. But even Kathy, who does have this extraordinary gift for the game, has reached the top and stayed there through determination and lots of hard work. Even though she's never done things quite the way people thought she should, she has been able to carry it off very well. Her natural feel has rescued her, time and time again. All the determination in the world could not have kept Kathy on top for so long had she not been blessed with this gift for feeling just what a golf club was doing as she moved it through her golf swing. Yet she still has to work on maintaining a golf swing to provide her with a medium through which she can express all of this ability. What you're aiming for in terms of a championship golfer is, ideally, someone who is gifted with a great amount of feel for the game and is willing to work very hard to take every advantage of his or her natural ability. And with all of the very talented people on both tours, I still don't know that there is anyone who is playing up to full potential. The people who are determined enough to put in all of the hard work are the ones that come the closest. They become and remain champions. There's no doubt that the finest players have a great deal of talent—but the thing about them that is most impressive is not so much their talent but their determination.

Life as a Tournament Player

I began playing in local junior tournaments around St. Louis when I was about seven, and continued my involvement in junior golf well on into my teens. Junior golf is a very important thing insofar as it helps to maintain an interest in the game beyond practice and casual play. Even if a young golfer expects to work for ten or fifteen years to train for a life in golf, it's difficult to keep up a reasonable level of enthusiasm unless there are events to look forward to and work toward. I always had two or three events every year that I tried to establish as goals for that particular year, and these helped a great deal in keeping my competitive spirits high. One of the most important things to be had from an association with junior golf competition is the development of a proper attitude. Golf's a character builder, and junior golf teaches a child to take the good with the bad, the bad with the good. It was a great help to me in my attempts to build a competitive game, since I was constantly reminded of the need for a proper outlook and a positive mental approach.

I joined the LPGA Tour when I was seventeen. When I first came out I was very much in awe of the entire business. It was scary. In almost no time at all I had lost most of the confidence in my game that I'd developed in the course of my junior career. I think that I was a good player as an amateur, and it doesn't seem, in retrospect, as though my game changed so drastically after I became a professional. It was almost uncanny, but somehow I simply lost my ability to perform as a golfer. I don't mean to say that I was horribly bad, but I never managed to do anything that was particularly impressive.

One of the things that may have hurt me as a young professional was that as a junior and teen-age player, I didn't lose very often—and when I did, it was mainly on account of some flash of stupidity on my part. Compared to that, the tour was a whole new ball game. I was encouraged by a lot of different people who told me that I had the ability to earn money out there and win. Yet I don't think that I ever really believed it. I had to get used to the fact that on given days there were a number of players who were simply going to beat me. I was very discouraged at first, and I got down on myself and my own future as a golfer. I can't say that there was no fun in it all—there were good times—but I played in only about nine tournaments that first year, and I was a little homesick, to tell the truth. Looking back, I see that I didn't quite have the powers of concentration then to perform much better than I actually did. I hit the ball very well in some of those early tournaments. I simply could not settle down enough to do anything with it as far as scoring was concerned. My age actually had a lot to do with it. I see girls come out on the tour now; some of them are very young and yet I haven't seen too many who are lacking in confidence. The entire atmosphere is different these days. The year that I came out there was a group of young players—Carol Mann, Sandra Haynie and myself—all just a year or two apart. We were in awe of the older, more established stars and suffered a lot when our games didn't measure up to theirs. It seems that the young players coming up today have adopted a different lifestyle. That's not to say that some of them don't work very hard on their games. They merely take things in stride much better. None of them appear to be in a frantic rush to get anywhere, and it takes some sort of catastrophe to get them down. They never seem to be discouraged. I think part of the confidence that new players have today stems from the fact that boys and girls seem to be maturing at an earlier age. Lately there has been a trend toward building up the newly emerging players much more than was the case when I was breaking in. A young player today can count on a rash of complimentary publicity if she has any reputation prior to joining the tour. And there are no new young players who have become greats as of yet. But the build-ups that they receive are good as far as their confidence is concerned. I don't believe that the new girls today have a greater knowledge or understanding of the game than we had back then. They just appear to have more success, in a shorter span of time, than we did. There are also many more girls coming out to play.

There is a good deal more incentive for the younger player these days to prepare for a career on the tour. There is much more to be gained by doing well on the women's tour now

than there was back in the early sixties. With the rise in popularity experienced by the LPGA in recent years, life for a young
player is somewhat more interesting. Expansion of media cov-
erage has increased the excitement surrounding each individual
tournament, and, as more people become familiar with women's
golf, the flavor of life out on the tour becomes more appealing.

When I started out on the tour, there were perhaps thirty
players, in all, competing. Now there are more than a hundred
at many tournament sites. The competition has become keener
as more girls are attracted by the rewards offered for success. The
marginal player cannot survive very well these days. The tour is
a bit more of a job now, and golf is a bit more like work. If you
let yourself down and don't perform well, you lose much more
in terms of potential reward. Although we may have been over-
ly dramatic in my early days, it always seemed to us as though
we had suffered a tremendous loss whenever something went
wrong. In a sense, we took things too seriously, and often we
would attack our problems from the wrong standpoint. But the
girls today are a different breed, and I'm certain that it's true
of the young players on the men's tour. They are studious and
very serious about their games, and yet they have an ability to
leave golf on the golf course and build a more diverse spectrum
of interests and activities. It was much more of a twenty-four-
hour-a-day thing with us in my early days. Our entire lives were
centered around golf, and our spirits rose and fell with our fortunes on the course. There was little else to turn to. Now it's
possible to play golf on the course and do other things away
from the course, which perhaps is a very healthy thing and explains most of the positive changes in the attitudes of young
people.

There were very few new players coming out at the time
I joined the tour, so in essence I was alone when I began. I

was fortunate in that there were enough young people out on tour for me to make some friends. Today there are many more players, both established players and emerging players, and it is not such a lonely place to be. Again, the young girls today have more people and more outside interests to turn to as a relief from the strain of competitive golf.

Even today, after fourteen years as a professional player, I find it difficult to leave my feelings on the golf course when the round is done. Sometimes I'll talk over a bad round with Yippy, my husband, and other times I'll go off by myself and sulk. Sulking is not a good thing for anyone, but I usually find that I don't make the same mistake twice. I tend to get very angry with myself and I want to be left alone, but often some good will emerge from it.

The most annoying rounds are the ones in which I've hit the ball well, putted reasonably well, stayed away from any serious blunders, and have still managed to shoot myself out of contention. Usually it's a matter of a few mental errors costing me a good round. Not too long ago I had such a round that was especially rankling: the day was perfect, the course was not that difficult, and I shot 74. Under those conditions, 74 was more like 78 relative to the remainder of the field. It sounds like a respectable score, but I could not have been more disgusted. And I didn't even fall down in one particular area of the game—I played many holes very well, even hit the pin twice during the round, and my putting was fair. But plain mental blunders had me off track early in the round and I never managed to recover from it. I got angry at myself and angry at the situation that I was in, I drove into a fairway bunker on a straightforward par 4, and although I wasn't too pleased with having driven the ball in the sand, I counted on having a relatively simple shot of about 120 yards out of the bunker to the green. Instead, the ball was up under the lip of the trap and I was faced with a difficult shot just trying to move the ball out of the sand. As I stood there and looked at that predicament, I simply wanted to explode, since the same thing had happened to me the week before. In the previous tournament I had played a very good shot down the first fairway, and I was in a position from which I could just about reach the green on this par 5 in two. There was a large trap right in front of the green, but that was of little consequence since I felt that I might be able to make a birdie even from the sand. So I just blasted one right at the green, thinking that even if I wound up in the trap it would be no big matter. Well, the ball went into the bunker, and when I reached it, it was sitting in this little area where there happened to be a natural wall built up. The ball was right up against this wall. There I was after hitting two good shots, after thinking out my game plan thoroughly, yet in a spot from which I couldn't even play out backwards. I almost broke my wrist trying to blast out. So when the exact same thing happened during the first round of the next week's tournament, I was what you might call quite irritated. I had these awful flashes of every shot that rolled into a trap finding its way into an unplayable lie. So I stood there, fuming and feeling sorry for myself—bad policy, since things of that sort are as they are and can't be changed after the fact. In any event, I did manage to scrape the ball out of that lie and make a bogey on the hole, which should not have been that disastrous. But I carried that resentment over my bad luck with me for another hole, and I made a second bogey and let the whole round go right down the drain … all because of my inability to think sensibly and regard everything from a proper perspective. The whole thing was merely the result of a mental error. And although you and I both will have some days like that, there was just no excuse for my attitude. None at all. Disastrous things happen many times on one hole, but I find that when I'm thinking well I can leave all my bad thoughts on that hole, and go on to the next with a clear head.

In any case, I do get very upset with myself when I'm not playing well, and if my problems appear to stem from a mistake in my swing pattern, then I become very concerned. Any good player is able to tell when he or she has struck the ball well simply by the feeling at impact. You know the feeling that you are striving for when trying to play a certain shot, and that feeling either emerges at impact or it does not. If you have to make adjustments in your swing to get the clubface on the ball, all is not well mechanically. When I play poorly for this reason, I worry a great deal about my swing, but I am not as upset as when I waste a day of potentially fine golf because of mental mistakes. I feel as though I'm a good player, but I don't like to spot the leaders six shots in the first round of a tournament. It's just not that easy.

I really have the same group of friends out on the tour that I've always had. I don't spend quite so much time with my friends now that I'm married and have a family. Marlene Hagge, Pam Higgins, and Carol Mann are all friends. There's a small group of us out there, and we've always spent a good bit of time together. Now I spend somewhat more time with Kathy Cornelius, because our children are nearly the same age and they've been together often.

There are very few people playing with me on the tour whom I allow to advise me regarding my golf swing. I don't even want to hear what anyone has to say on the matter. Unsolicited advice sometimes raises questions in your mind about your own swing, and doubts are the last thing that *anyone* needs out here. I might, from time to time, ask a friend to check and see where I'm aiming. But I wouldn't allow anyone to work on the character of my own particular swing. That's simply the way I feel about it, and I've had more or less the same sentiments ever since I came on tour. If I do feel as though I'm getting into serious trouble where my swing is concerned, the best thing for me is to leave the tour and try to find the problem. And that's when I go to my father. We always revert to the fundamental ideas that have been so important to my game throughout the years. We can generally pick out one aspect of my action that seems not to be working properly at the time, such as a smooth takeaway or a good turn. Many times when I've felt as though I was hitting the ball tolerably well my father has caught the beginning symptoms of a basic flaw, and worked with me to correct it. As I gain experience, I am getting better at helping myself with some of the problems. Still, you're never able to see yourself while you are making a correction. You can only proceed by feel and results. It's very reassuring to have someone around to act as a mirror, someone who knows your swing inside-out, someone you trust. At times, when I'm on the course and seemingly hitting the ball well, I find that all of a sudden I'm not getting as much distance as I should. Out on the course, where I have to do my own repair work, one little change like checking to see that I'm extending the club to make a big arc to the top can bring back that lost power during the course of a round. Most of the learning that I do now is a matter of returning to the good simple things that have always been with me. I don't waste much time hunting for something new.

A Winning Edge

To win on the professional tour, you must feel as though you are capable of winning. Remember that only you can control what you do. You must have a certain amount of confidence in your abilities as a golfer. In a sense, you have to be somewhat self-centered to become a winner—at least insofar as your golf game is concerned. The top players never seem to worry about their fellow competitor's games; they have enough faith in their own abilities to forget about what's going on about them and settle down to the task of winning.

Winners appear to play their best golf while under pressure, and that's a function of a person's ability to dispense with all sorts of conscious thought and allow the automatic pilot—"muscle memory"—to assume control. This is not to say that the victor is not nervous or that the player who is in strong contention during the final few holes does not feel the pressure. They are merely able to control themselves, and they can function skillfully under the circumstances. People often forget that pressure is strictly an internal commodity, a person's own interior response to the situation at hand. At times you hear people speaking of pressure as though it were a tangible entity, when in fact it has no more substance than anger or fear or joy. Pressure is a product of your own mind and, as such, can be controlled and dealt with readily if you are willing to devote your mind to the effort. It takes some mental training. I do believe that some personalities by nature are more emotional than others—maybe myself included. This makes the job of controlling your mind a little tougher.

The best players in golf always give the impression that they are in complete control at all times, that they are the masters of their own destinies. Even when they don't win they leave you with the feeling that they have done all that was possible under the circumstances, that they didn't allow a bad attitude to ruin a round. If a talented golfer is able to give his or her best effort every time out, that golfer will eventually come out on top. It will be just a matter of time before things fall into place.

As much as some people will deny the importance of luck as an influence in championship golf, I think that luck does play a certain role in determining the winner of any particular tournament. Actually, it's not so much a question of good luck but rather the avoidance of any bad luck, if you catch the distinction. At times your ability can carry you through without any unusually lucky things helping you along, but very bad luck is something that I find ruinous. When all conditions are the same for all players, half an inch can determine who wins and who does not. You can plug up in the bank of a trap or you can barely clear it and roll all the way to the hole. You can be the greatest player in the game and yet I'm certain that you can't control the flight of a golf ball to a degree of inches. I'm not after any extraordinary good luck, but I'm always hoping that I can avoid the very bad things, things that you don't ordinarily take into account when considering the risk involved in playing a given shot, such as a bird flying into your ball and causing it to drop in a pond (to use an extreme example). During one tournament in Los Angeles I had a 6- or 7-iron into a green and the pin was tucked way over on the right corner. At this particular tournament the gallery ropes came right up to the edge of the green rather than flaring out as they normally do. I hit a very good shot and the ball was floating right down at the flag, looking like a near-perfect stroke … but instead of dropping near the hole, the ball hit one of the gallery ropes dead in the center and rebounded way off the green. I had nearly a full wedge left to get back. That's what I mean by bad luck. When you hit the ball into a bunker and it sticks up under a lip, you've had a touch of bad luck. The intended penalty for hitting into a sand trap is generally based on the simple fact that you'll have to play your next shot from sand. Sand traps were not designed with the intention of giving you an unplayable lie. So when I do get an unplayable lie in the sand, I consider myself somewhat less than fortunate. It may well be true that the good luck balances the bad in the long run, but it seems that the winner of any single tournament has generally not had much bad luck. Things have more or less gone according to schedule. In any event, when you adopt an attitude about luck, remember that the root cause of anything that happens to your golf ball is *you*. You hit it to begin with. That's the only thing that you can do, physically, to influence the outcome of a shot, so it's the only thing that you should worry about. Stay calm and resolute, and let the chips fall as they may.

The Colgate-European Open at Sunningdale, England was without a doubt one of my biggest wins ever. My key thought throughout that tournament was to place the ball in the fairway, because Sunningdale is a brutal course if you are not keeping the ball in play. It was one of those weeks when I found myself swinging very well, so all I had to concentrate on was making solid contact, hitting the ball clearly and off the center of the clubface. I was thinking about that down to the very last shot at Sunningdale, and it worked beautifully for me. I was really hitting the ball with a great deal of control and confidence. There was one particular shot on the last day that I remember as being a good illustration of this point. The sixteenth hole was a very long par 4, and with the wind in our faces, as it was during the final round, there was no way that it could be reached in two shots. There were fairway bunkers sitting about fifty yards in front of the green up on a little hill, so that if you find them you are left with a very difficult shot into the green. I was play-ing with Betsy Cullen, and Betsy hit what appeared to be a very good second shot, but she still couldn't get over the sand. I had driven a bit longer, and I had a downhill lie. I knew that I was leading at this point, but I didn't know my margin. So I had a pretty important decision to make with the second shot. At the time, this seemed to be a key hole for me. I knew that I could not hit a high shot, because the wind would blow it right back in my face, and a low shot would never carry the bunkers going up the hill. I suppose that, in fact, I was faced with the prospect of either hitting a nearly perfect 3-wood or playing my third shot from the sand. I decided to play the 3-wood, and the sole thought in my mind at the time was to make precise contact. I hit about as good a shot as I ever have, and the ball cleared the bunkers nicely and left me with a very easy little chip to the hole. That may have clinched the tournament right there. With all of the long fairway shots to play over there, the simple thought of meeting the ball solidly and staying with the shot— being conscious of the clubhead following the ball out toward the target—helped me immeasurably. In this most complex of games, it's simple things that count toward winning.

Despite her petite frame, Judy developed a swing that made her one of the longest hitters in golf during her career. She believes that swinging must be a fluid motion or "disciplined freedom," and she teaches that, "If you stand over the ball for more than a couple of seconds before you begin your swing, you must keep in motion. Whether that means getting your feet set right or making a little waggle of the club. Gentle motion keeps you from becoming tense."

My Personal Revelation

Vivien Saunders
from *The Golfing Mind*, 1984

Born in England, Vivien Saunders was the first European woman to obtain her player's card for the American tour, and in 1971 she was the first non-American to qualify at the LPGA teaching exams. She was later known to have a particular talent for coaching and encouraging young players.

By the time she was twenty, she had set six course records and was well on her way to establishing an impressive golfing career. As an amateur she won numerous tournaments and came in second in the 1966 Ladies' British Open Amateur Championship. After turning professional in 1969, she won the Ladies' British Open Championship in 1977 and spent her time in America playing golf, teaching, and writing. She published several golf books, including The Golfing Mind *from which the essay below is taken.*

I am certain that the greatest transformation in my own game of golf, both as player and as teacher, came about through realizing one particular point: a game of golf is made up of a number of totally separate shots. I began to appreciate that producing a good score was simply a matter of stringing together as many good shots and as few bad shots as possible. But what I also realized was that I and almost every other golfer, both amateur and professional, viewed these shots as being linked in some way, so that one shot was allowed to affect another. I began to look at my own golf more critically and saw that my mental approach to shots varied quite unnecessarily. I could see, for example, that I had a different attitude towards a fairway wood to the green on a short par five than towards a fairway wood on a long par four; I approached the shot in a different way if I was scoring badly than if I was leading the field. I realized that I had yet another different approach if I had perhaps driven into the trees, chipped out and was in some way trying to make up for my previous error. On closely analyzing my game I found that this occurred with every type of shot. The chip or pitch where I was struggling to make par was somehow more pressured than the one where I had a good chance of making a birdie. The four-foot putt for a two was not approached in the same way as a four-foot putt for a six.

What I immediately discovered was that this was detrimental to my game. And then I looked at others, those I watched and those I taught, and it became obvious that most of them were affected in exactly the same way as I was, the club golfer suffering unnecessary disasters and a professional like myself failing to capitalize fully from his or her own potential. And then I also began to learn that a few players possessed the gift or acquired the discipline—I'm not sure which—of being able to see each particular golf shot as an entirely separate task. I realized that this single-minded, concentrated approach enabled them to attack each shot in virtually the same way, whether winning or losing, competing or not competing, playing at home or abroad, struggling for a bogey or hoping for an eagle. In fact I discovered that when taken to extremes they no longer struggled for bogeys or hoped for eagles but simply concentrated on each shot in a totally detached manner.

With this realization I became determined not only to learn

this ability myself but to indoctrinate my pupils with the same discipline. Learning this "single-shot technique" was by no means easy. Even now, I suppose I catch myself with the odd stray thought but invariably bring my attention back on track. But the very day I started trying to learn the technique my golf improved. I began to be able to look at shots in a far more detached and rational way. I would think to myself, "Here I am trying to hit this ball from A to B with a 5-iron." My concentration improved, I began to be able to ignore what had gone before, how I was scoring, and so on. Having played that shot I would then forget about it, whether good or bad, as quickly as possible and walk to wherever the ball might be, approaching the next shot in exactly the same uncomplicated way. I began to lose the disastrous urge to try to make up for previous errors or thinking of what lay ahead. I found a game of golf far less mentally strenuous—I suppose because my concentration became centered around each shot, thus casting out unnecessary and presumably burdensome thoughts.

My mental approach to golf changed dramatically. By seeing the game as being purely and simply made up of a number of single, self-contained shots I was beginning to manage not only to approach each shot with the same mental attitude but to cast errors out of my mind with far greater ease. Since I no longer dwelt on bad shots, they were no longer allowed to affect me. I began to play a totally new mental game on the course, which not only made each game become much more satisfying but also made me a better golfer. My new mental approach required me to play each shot to the best of my ability regardless of the score, the nature of the competition, the opposition, and so on. I would think to myself, "Supposing I was just demonstrating this in a clinic, talking through the shot with my audience." What in turn followed from this was that my own satisfaction from each shot came not only from how close the ball landed to the hole but also from pleasure at my own composure and undistracted thoughts. In this way the external performance became almost less important than the internal one. In some ways I derived greater satisfaction from perfect mental control of the game than I did from the actual score. I realized that with perfecting this technique I would virtually conquer the mental game of golf.

Almost every golfer, whether amateur or professional, falls into the trap of seeing shots as being linked together so that one shot is allowed to affect another. Except among those who are exceptionally well disciplined in the way I have described above, the golfer will invariably try to make up for what has gone before, either trying to recover from a poor shot by taking unjustifiable risks or by pressurizing himself to make a birdie to recover from a dropped shot. The disciplined training you must have is to see the game of golf as made up of a number of totally separate shots, so that the mind is simply focused for any particular shot on playing that shot to the best of your ability. The object is simply to strike the ball from A to B. There is no question of trying to make up for what has gone before or of compensating for errors.

Vivian Saunders believes that "the very nature of the game means that any momentary loss of concentration or confidence can see a champion coming unstuck." But she teaches that, "Concentration and decision-making have to be highly developed to repel any momentary weakness, while the level of confidence has to be finely tuned somewhere between foolish arrogance and a wise humility for accepting inevitable imperfections."

Pressure Golf

Jane Blalock
from *The Guts to Win*, 1977

Jane Blalock was one of the most consistent players on the LPGA Tour. After having an excellent amateur career—winning the New Hampshire amateur title four consecutive times from 1965-1968, the Florida Intercollegiate, and the New England amateur—she turned professional and joined the LPGA Tour in 1969. Just one year later, Jane won her first tour championship at the Atlanta Carling Open. She continued to play in 299 events without missing a cut—a record yet to broken by any touring professional, female or male. She also accumulated an impressive twenty-nine tournament wins between 1970 and 1985.

After retiring, Jane Blalock formed her own company and, among many things, conducts LPGA golf clinics nationwide. Currently she manages the Women's Legend Tour.

In her inspirational book, The Guts to Win, *Jane gives her no-nonsense advice on matters of golf. Here she describes how she deals with playing under pressure.*

We all suffer and sweat in the crunch of competition. Not long ago I was playing a social round in Florida with a lady friend, an amateur with a handicap of about 20. We had a little wager going—$2 for each nine, with strokes. On the 17th green she looked nervously at a six-foot putt, stepped back and groaned. "Oh, this is awful," she said. "My stomach is like a knot. You're so fortunate, Janie. On the tour you must face these problems so often they don't bother you."

Is she kidding?

I've been in situations on the tour where I was scared to death. My stomach had butterflies, my legs were rubbery, my hands felt clammy and my mouth was so dry it felt like the morning after an all-night party. I recall many times when the tension was so great my jawbone was quivering, and I found myself gnashing my teeth audibly.

Professional or amateur, no golfer is ever immune to pressure. How do we overcome it?

I've tried just about everything. Golf is really a cruel game. In football you can release your frustrations by crashing into somebody. In tennis you can put that extra juice on a forehand or rush the net. In golf you don't have those options.

The best ways I know to combat tension are to do deep knee bends on the tee, or shake your hands vigorously before taking the shot. That gets the blood flowing again and loosens the knots. On the greens, sometimes I pace around to inspect the putt from all angles. I don't actually see anything, but it looks like I know what I'm doing and sometimes it takes my mind off the importance of the putt.

Once you're in the furnace however, the best thing to have going for you is a fierce desire to win. In eight years on the tour, I've had more than my share of tight finishes. Sometimes I pulled it out, sometimes I didn't, but I remember each one vividly. You learn from those experiences, especially when you lose.

I'll never forget the Women's Civitan Open at Dallas in 1973. I lost it because the pressure got to me and restricted my swing, costing me a tournament I should have won.

I was defending champion at Dallas that year, having beaten Kathy Whitworth in that acrimonious playoff in 1972. Kathy was playing well in this one, too, leading the tournament. With five holes remaining in the final round, I was only one stroke behind. I was sure I could catch her.

On the 14th hole, I had a 10-foot putt for a birdie that looked so simple my mind was envisioning the ball dropping in before I stroked it. But the putt lipped out. On the 15th hole, I had a 15-footer for a birdie, hit it perfectly and missed. Time was running out.

Standing on the 16th fairway, about 115 yards from the green, I asked my caddie for the pin placement. "Front center," he replied. I hit a 9-iron shot to the front center. Unfortunately, my caddie was wrong. The pin was placed toward the back of the green, leaving me a putt of 30 feet.

Anxious and upset, I charged the putt and hit it four feet past the pin. Then I missed it coming back. Bogey. I could feel my nerves waxing raw and edgy.

On the 17th hole, I had a downhill approach shot of 140 yards. Normally, I'd hit an 8-iron in that situation. I guess I wasn't thinking very clearly because I took a 7-iron, then made a terrible swing. I did what so many amateurs do under stress: I failed to complete the backswing. I pulled the shot and the ball bounded off a mound to the left of the green. I bogeyed that hole, too, and lost by a stroke.

The moral of that story is that under pressure you must make absolutely sure you complete your backswing. Take the club back slowly, extend the arms fully and hesitate a moment at the top before starting the downswing. In other words, don't hurry the swing.

For the pure agony of sustained tension, I don't suppose I've ever experienced anything like the 1974 Colgate-Dinah Shore tournament at Mission Hills. It was the most exciting day of my career, and the fact it was on national television only heightened the drama—and the pressure.

With nine holes to play on the final round, I was six strokes behind Sandra Haynie, who was with me in the last threesome, and four behind Jo Ann Prentice, in the group ahead. I picked up a stroke with a thirty-foot birdie putt on the 10ᵗʰ hole, and chipped in on 12. On the 17ᵗʰ, a par-3, I hit my tee shot one foot from the pin. When first Jo Ann and then Sandra bogeyed that hole, I was only one stroke behind them both going into 18, a par-5 with water surrounding the green.

I tried to think only of taking the club back slowly and staying down through the ball on the drive, and I hit it solidly. After a good 4-wood second shot, I was left with a 9-iron to the green. I made a perfect swing, extending the clubhead straight through at the target, and hit the ball five feet from the flag.

In the ABC television tower behind the green, Dave Marr made a friendly $1 bet with Cathy Duggan, one of our tour players who was doing TV commentary, that I would miss the putt.

"You don't know Janie," Cathy replied, and the bet was on. I didn't take much time lining up that putt. I stroked it crisply, accelerating my left hand through the ball, it fell in for a birdie. Dave Marr signed that dollar bill for Cathy.

Off the three of us went to the 14ᵗʰ hole for the start of a sudden death playoff. We were still on network television, and you think there wasn't a little sweating as we teed it up? I was so nervous I could hardly get the club back. We all got our pars on 14. On 15, I hit a 4-iron approach shot fifteen feet above the hole. Sandra and Jo Ann were both on the fringe. Sandra left her putt six feet short and Jo Ann rolled hers five feet past. Standing over my putt, I told myself, "Don't charge it." It was a dangerous downhill putt. I nudged the ball within two inches of the cup. Sandra missed to fall out of the playoff, but Jo Ann made hers.

On the 16th, a strong par-4 hole, I hit a long drive and put a 6-iron shot on the green, 25 feet away. Jo Ann's tee shot flew into a tree, but the ball caromed back onto the fairway. She smacked a 3-wood to the back fringe of the green. Two more pars, and on to 17.

The 17th is a difficult par-3 requiring a long iron. Jo Ann, who had the honor, hit a super shot, four feet from the flag. Now the pressure was on me. I wanted desperately to hit mine inside of Jo Ann's ball, but it finished 12 feet away. I missed the putt. There was nothing I could do except stand there and watch Jo Ann putt. She knocked it in, and it was all over.

In the confusion that followed, with the gallery scrambling around us, Jo Ann and I never did get around to shaking hands. That was interpreted by some as a sign of animosity between us. It wasn't the case at all. I tried to reach Jo Ann and congratulate her, but I was unable to because of the crush of traffic and the general chaos.

The two of us had a sequel later in the year, at the Lady Errol Classic in Apopka, Fla. I came from behind again, with birdies on 10, 11, 12 and 17, to tie Jo Ann and set up another sudden-death playoff. We both had the feeling we had been there before.

I won that playoff on the first extra hole, with a downhill birdie putt of 15 feet. This time I made sure there would be no repetition of the incident at Palm Springs. I walked over to Jo Ann, took her out-stretched hand and shook it heartily so everyone could see.

Sudden-death playoffs are searing on the nervous system. At the completion of regulation play, there is always a lot of confusion and excitement. Everyone's running around shouting. I try to get away by myself for a few moments before the playoff gets underway, but we generally have only about five minutes because it's late in the day and darkness is closing in.

One of the most memorable playoffs I was ever involved in took place in the 1975 Colgate Triple Crown at Mission Hills. It was the climax of a long and hectic struggle merely to qualify for the tournament.

The Triple Crown is the most exclusive event in women's golf. Only nine of the top players are invited to compete, based on their performance in three Colgate-sponsored tournaments: the Dinah Shore, the European Open, and the Far East Open. We play it at Mission Hills. It's only 36 holes, and the last round is nationally televised.

To qualify for the 1975 Triple Crown, held in December, I had to play well in the Far East Open in Australia the previous week. I shot 73 the first round and 74 the second, which placed me in a borderline qualifying position going into the final round. The critical hole on the last day was the 12th. I had chipped 15 feet past the flag, and as I waited my turn to putt, I had a little heart-to-heart talk with myself. "You didn't travel 15,000 miles to blow your chance," I said, "You're going to have to make this putt." I tried to remember the fundamentals of a good putting stroke, and I holed it. I made two birdies coming in and finished sixth in the overall compilation of the three tournaments, good enough for a ticket to Mission Hills.

In the first round of the Triple Crown I shot 71, one stroke behind the leader, JoAnne Carner. In the second and final round I was paired with Sandra Palmer and Carol Mann. Carner, Joann Washam, and Judy Rankin were in the threesome behind us. I was moving along smoothly until we reached the 14th, a par-3 with water on the right and out-of-bounds on the left. It's one of the most difficult par-3 holes I've seen.

Instead of playing the hole carefully, as I did the first round when I took a bogey, I attacked it. On the tee I looked down at the ball and said, "Little fellow, you're going for a ride." I hit a crisp iron shot and got my par, a real accomplishment for me on the hole.

On the 15th tee I noticed that Carner, Rankin, and Washam were all two under par for the tournament. I was one under. On the 17th another tough par-3, I made my best swing of the year. Remembering to complete the backswing, which is never all that easy under pressure, I hit a perfect 3-iron shot that finished eight feet from the cup. I made the putt, and even though I missed a 10-foot birdie putt on 18 that would have won the tournament right there, I finished in a three-way tie for the lead with Carner and Rankin.

We went into a sudden-death playoff. Talk about pressure! I can think of easier ways to earn a paycheck. JoAnne Carner and Judy Rankin are as tough and competitive as any two athletes anywhere. On the first playoff hole after the customary hectic five-minute wait, I hit a good drive and then a really fine 6-iron shot that wound up 12 feet from the flag. JoAnne and Judy each missed their birdie putts. Now it was up to me.

The line was dead straight. It was late in the day, so the grass was heavy. My only thought was, "Hit it firmly." The ball rolled in, and through the tears in my eyes I looked for my mom and dad in the gallery. It was a wonderful finish to the day, and to the year.

I have described some situations where a competitive temperament has helped me immeasurably, and I already know what you're thinking. How does someone acquire such a characteristic? How do I force myself to meet a challenge successfully?

Well, you've got to remember that I can't make every putt I want. If I did, I'd win every tournament. But there are times, crucial times, when I can concentrate so completely that it seems like I'm willing the ball into the hole. I've always been a good last-round player, and I'm proud of my record of winning the tournaments I have been in a position to win.

My background suggests that I had a competitive nature long before I began playing golf. This has been an asset, but I've gone beyond that to develop a sense of willpower that has created a reservoir of confidence in the crucible of a close finish.

An example was the Colgate Triple Crown held in January, 1977. I was the defending champion, based on my victory in December, 1975, and I was determined to win it again. Not only for the prestige, the cash, and the new Plymouth Volare station wagon, but also to launch my 1977 tour on a high note.

For three days before the tournament, I built myself into a state of emotional readiness. I was psyching myself up, mentally preparing for the competition. Not everybody can do that. I'm fortunate that I can. I'm not very good company during this time. I like to stay secluded, with no distractions or frivolities.

The end result is that I virtually *will* myself into a trance. I call it a mellow feeling. No highs, no lows. It's like I'm in a world of my own. I walk slowly, and try to keep my emotions on an even keel. I get angry on the course over a bad shot, sure, but I'm not about to display it by slamming my club to the ground or kicking the tee marker.

Despite that protective shroud, my emotions can still be boiling inside. I played consistent golf in the 1977 Triple Crown, but on the 16th hole of the final round I made a terrible first putt that left me with a five-footer for my par. I was scared. My caddie, Paul English, started to advise me on the putt but I cut him off with the remark, "No, let me handle it." That putt was the most crucial stroke I had, and I made it. I didn't need to make a birdie on 18 to win, but I felt mellow enough that if I had to, I could.

Speaking of pressure situations, I'd like to bring up a point I've often heard discussed among good athletes. It's a little-known fact that the most critical time in a competition, the real moment of truth, may often occur early in the day. Nobody else might recognize it, but the turning point is there. If you pull it off, the other pieces fall into place. If you don't, you know it's going to be an uphill battle.

Joan Joyce, the softball pitcher, says that for her the critical point comes in the first inning of the game. She wants desperately to shut the other team out in the first inning, with three strikeouts, if possible. It gives her an edge. Billie Jean King says her crucial time in tennis is the seventh game of a set. My own pivotal hole varies. It may be the second, or the 12th, as it was during the Triple Crown qualifying in Australia. But I can always recognize when the time has come, when I must bear down harder.

I've often wondered if the Oakland Raiders felt that way in the first period of the 1977 Super Bowl, when they recovered a Minnesota fumble on their own two-yard line. The Raiders took command of the game at that point, and the Vikings looked like a beaten team.

I'm a football fan, and as I sat there in the Rose Bowl and watched while Oakland built a substantial lead, I thought back to my own experience in the Dallas tournament in 1976. It's always a strain to lead during the final round, and the pressure can be compounded when you lead it all the way. Occasionally, however, your tempo is so good that you just blow everyone else right out of the ball park. That happened in Dallas, where I won the tournament by nine strokes.

There is no middle ground for me in my feeling for a course. I either love it or I hate it. My record shows that I play certain courses very well, others very poorly. I've won three times at Mission Hills and twice each at Indian Hills, Errol Estate, and Brookhaven. Brookhaven, the site of the Dallas tournament, is definitely one of my favorite courses. It is well designed and appealing, requires a strong mid-iron game and the greens are true.

The background of my 1976 Dallas victory is hardly a model of proper tournament preparation. I wouldn't suggest it as a regular diet, but in this case it must have been just right for me.

The tournament preceding Dallas was the Jerry Lewis Muscular Dystrophy Classic at the Rail Golf Club in Springfield, Illinois. I wound up in a four-way playoff that went three holes before Sandra Palmer finally won. I finished fifth, three strokes behind the leaders. I wanted to spend a few days in New England before going down to Dallas, and since there was no commercial flight out of Springfield on Sunday night, Carol Mann and I chartered a plane to Chicago. It cost us $125 apiece, but it was worth it. I flew into Hartford that night and then drove on to Meridian (Connecticut) to be with our softball team for a few days.

It was a relaxing time, watching the girls practice and play softball, and I didn't leave until Wednesday morning on the five-hour flight from Hartford to Dallas. I got there just in time to play in the pro-am. Brookhaven has 36 holes, and the pro-am was played at the course we did not use for the tournament. It rained all Thursday morning. I got out late that afternoon and played nine holes. I didn't putt the greens, because they had been softened by the rain and I knew they'd be firmer the next day. So I teed it up on Friday with a minimum of preparation.

Although I was physically tired from all the traveling, my mental attitude was good. The pressure is always stronger until you win your first tournament of the year, and I had won at

Wheeling, West Virginia, a few weeks earlier, so I was loose and confident. My only thought on the first tee in the opening round was this: "Today, I'm not going to start out with any 76 and spot the field nine shots. I've had enough of those shaky first rounds. Today, the field is going to spot me nine shots." I birdied the first hole, picked up four birdies on the back nine and shot 67. I didn't have a nine-stroke lead, but I had four, over Sandra Post, and that's not a bad start.

The next day I birdied the first hole again. I was hitting everything into the hole. I made four birdie putts of more than 10 feet, and par putts of four, six, eight, and 10 feet. Now I was pulling away from the field. I shot another 67 and had my nine-stroke lead. It was the first time I had ever played two straight competitive rounds without a bogey.

Coming down the back nine on that second round, I kept thinking, "Just keep whittling away. Be tough. When you've got somebody down, stomp on them. The greater cushion you can build today, the easier things will be tomorrow."

It was like Raymond Floyd at the 1976 Masters. The only way he could have lost on the final day was to collapse completely, and then someone else still would have needed an exceptional round to catch him. I was nervous that Saturday night, though. Kathy Whitworth was 10 strokes behind me; I knew she'd be making a real run the next day.

So the pressure was there, even with a nine-shot lead. I was very shaky early in the final round. I scuffed a wedge shot over the first green and had to make a six-foot putt to save par. On the fifth green I three-putted from twenty-five feet, my first bogey in 40 holes. I took bogeys on the ninth and 10th, both tough holes into the wind, but I still led by seven with eight holes to play. Something like Palmer at Olympic in the '66 Open? I didn't want to think about that.

Well, it was one of those days. I shot birdies on 11, 12, 13, and 14 and that was it. Kathy Whitworth's 70 was the low round of the day, which gave her second place at 214, but I shot 71 for a 205 and the nine-stroke win. It was by far my best performance of the year. Later I checked my biorhythm chart for that week, and everything was a strong plus. No wonder I felt so great.

People asked me after that tournament if there was anything that a golfer trailing by nine shots can do to break the leader's momentum. Can a little gamesmanship come into play? Sometimes it can, but not that day. The only thing anyone could have done was try to birdie every hole and hope I would have nothing but trouble. There's not much they could have said.

I do remember one time at St. Paul in 1973, when Sandra Palmer said something to me that influenced the final outcome. It was a much closer finish than Dallas. Sandra had a two-shot lead going into the final round, but after shooting 32 on the front nine I led by two. On the 10th tee Sandra turned to me and said, "You're sure making a lot of good putts." It might have been an intentional effort to disrupt my concentration. I got to the 10th green and began thinking, "Gee, I have been making some good putts." I hadn't been concerned about how I made them, I just had a good putting rhythm. Suddenly that rhythm was gone. Sandra won the tournament.

If that ever happens to me again, I'll just smile and say, "I'm going to keep on making them"—and hope that I do.

That kind of tactic is probably more widespread in match play, a game most of the tour women hate. We don't play much of it and that's just as well. Match play is a personal thing. You're trying to eliminate your opponent, send her on down the road. Feelings can easily become strained.

In match play, every hole is like a sudden-death playoff. I've seen experienced pros get so tense they begin to almost hyperventilate. When that happens, you must pull yourself aside, take some deep breaths and drink some water to wash down that cotton-dry feeling.

My first experience at match play on the tour was such a calamity it left me scarred for months. It was the 1972 Sears Women's Classic at Port St. Lucie, Florida, our only match play event of that year. I was leading Betsy Cullen 2-up with three holes to play. I shot them in two pars and a birdie. The only problem was that Betsy finished birdie-birdie-eagle. She beat me with a long putt on 18. I was so crushed I swore I'd never again enter a match play tournament, but eventually the pain wore off.

Much more satisfying was the 1976 International Team Mixed Championship, sponsored by Trans-World International and played in Ireland. Teams composed of men and women professionals represented the United States, England, South Africa, and Australia. Raymond Floyd and I were the U.S. entry. It wasn't match play in the strictest sense of the term, but rather what they call stroke match. For example, team A plays team B, the loser dropping out and the winner advancing. The result is not determined hole by hole, but by the number of strokes. It combines features of both games.

Our first match was against Graham Marsh and Jan Stephenson, the Australian team. They are both great players. Raymond and I were four strokes down after the first seven holes at Waterville, but we caught up and eventually won that match by a stroke. In the finals we moved to Killarney and met the South African tigers, Gary Player and Sally Little. We won by eight strokes.

Having some Irish blood in me, it was a wonderful experience playing over there. The people were warm and gracious, and the courses excellent. It was an ideal week's break in the middle of the summer.

Even though we played those matches in total strokes instead of hole by hole, it had a close resemblance to the dominant type of competition for club tournaments, because one bad hole doesn't have to cost the whole round.

There's always tension, though, and it seems to increase when handicap strokes are involved. The woman who receives the stroke feels she must come through because of the advantage. You've heard the old line, "Partner, you've got a stroke on this one, so make it count." Brrr. I can just see the muscles stiffening. One bad shot breeds another. Instead of coming directly out of trouble and settling for a bogey—a net par which will probably win the hole—the stroke recipient gambles on a heroic shot through the trees and winds up with an eight.

If you start feeling tense, try to slow down your tempo. Walk slower, and take a more leisurely backswing. Avoid the mistake of standing over the ball at address too long. That just promotes more strain. We have a saying on tour, "Let her fly." It's something to remember when you're trying to steer the ball around the course in an attempt to keep it in play. Relax, and enjoy the game.

No matter how hard you try to overcome battle nerves, the very structure of tournament golf creates an atmosphere of stress within us all. One day I was playing a social round in Boca Raton with Mrs. Hoe Wolfel, whose husband is an engineer for Pro-Dyne, a golf equipment company. She got to talking about how nervous she becomes in club tournaments.

"My hands get so clammy," she said, "I actually hate to shake hands with my opponent after a round. It's embarrassing." I told her that we have the same problem on the tour, on every hole of every round of the year.

Concentration, so vital to good golf, is another problem in club competition. It's tough to concentrate while you're inquiring about your partner's children, or what you're going to have for dinner that night. There are times when you just have to ignore those distractions.

I was talking about this on the course one day with Carl Yastrzemski of the Boston Red Sox. (Carl threw a 79 at me with a 14 handicap). I asked him how he could concentrate at bat while some of those Fenway Park fans were booing him.

"By blocking them out of my mind." He replied, "I don't even hear them. When I'm going good they cheer and when I'm in a slump they boo. I just don't pay any attention. It's me and the pitcher out there, and the only thing I'm concentrating on is the ball coming in."

Yastrzemski is one of the most competitive persons I've ever known. In the clutch, he's at his best.

I'd like to share with you a poem that I refer to often when the going gets tough. I clipped it out of a magazine and keep it in my golf bag.

> If you think you are beaten,
> You are.
> If you think you dare not,
> You don't.
> If you'd like to win,
> But think you can't,
> It's almost a cinch you won't.
> If you think you'll lose,
> You're lost.
> For in this world we find
> Success begins with a fellow's will;
> It's all in the state of mind.
> Life's battles don't always go
> To the stronger or fleeter man;

But sooner or later the man who wins
Is the one who thinks he can.

Jane Blalock was known as one of the most competitive players on tour. After a stunning start on the LPGA Tour, she suffered a few mediocre years. However, in 1985 she came back to have one of her best seasons ever, winning the Women's Kemper Open and the Mazda Japan Classic. She has always taught that you should give your golf game your best but never think that your whole livelihood is riding on your next shot.

Taking on Tournament Challenges

Amy Alcott
from *Amy Alcott's Guide to Women's Golf,* 1991

Amy Alcott is one of the most charismatic and accomplished women golfers in the world. She has won nearly every major women's golf tournament and has over thirty professional wins to her credit. Her five majors include: the 1979 Peter Jackson Classic, the 1983, 1988, and 1991 Nabisco-Dinah Shore Winner's Circle, and the United States Women's Open, which she won by nine stokes. Her golfing career began at a young age when she practiced hitting balls into a net in her backyard and putting balls into soup cans. She joined the LPGA Tour just two weeks after her eighteenth birthday, and she went on to win at least one tournament each season from 1975 to 1986. In 1999, she was inducted into the LPGA Hall of Fame.

Winning Under Diversity: The 1980 U.S. Open

I guess I'd have to say that winning the 1980 U.S. Open was one of the most satisfying victories, both because it's our national championship and because I won it under such difficult conditions. We played at Richland Country Club in Nashville, and the temperature neared 110 degrees each day. A reporter asked Marlene Hagge who she thought would win and Marlene answered, "Whoever finishes." She wasn't far from the truth, in that we had ten players who withdrew because the heat and humidity was just too intense.

I knew that the key to playing well was going to be patience. I just had to believe that everybody was suffering as much as I was, and I knew that if I could just keep my wits about me I had a good chance of winning.

I never hit more than ten balls before a round. I kept covering my head with cool, wet towels, and I stayed in the shade as much as possible. Still, on the last day I didn't really think I could hang on. I don't remember much about the front nine, but on the 9th green I began to feel delirious. I came close to passing out.

I knew I had a very comfortable nine-shot lead, and I began talking to myself. "Amy, you used to putt into tin cans and pretend they were for the U.S. Open. You may never have this chance again. Just hang in. Please, just hang in and let the chips fall where they may. Just don't give up."

I walked as slowly as I could for the rest of the round. My hands were so swollen they felt like baseball mitts. I had no feel at all, but I did have a big lead and so I tried to just play one shot at a time.

As I came to the last hole, a 360-yard par 4, I knew that if I could just hang on I'd win. I had a ten-shot lead over Hollis Stacy, and she wasn't in any better condition than I was.

I topped my drive, but instead of becoming flustered I just decided to do whatever I could to finish the hole. I hit and 8-iron, followed by a 9-iron to within 25 feet of the hole. As we approached the green, Hollis looked at me and said, "Don't fifteen-putt."

The lesson is that when you're playing in bad conditions, try to keep on an even keel and remember that everyone is in the same position. I don't mind playing under adversity (it's my nickname, Amy Adversity) because I think it gives me an edge—although I never want to play in conditions like that again.

Play Your Own Game:
The 1981 Bent Tree Ladies Classic

I've always enjoyed testing myself against the best players. That's one reason I joined the LPGA Tour right out of high school; it's one reason I've always liked coming down the stretch against JoAnne Carner. I know that if I beat her, I've beaten the best.

That's just what happened in the 1981 Bent Tree Ladies' Classic in Sarasota. We were paired in the final round, and I took a one-stroke lead on 17 when she missed a short putt. The 18th is a reachable par 5 guarded by two ponds, one to the right in the landing area, and another guarding the front left of the green. I hit a good drive down the middle of the fairway, but JoAnne killed her drive. I didn't have any real choice but to lay up. I didn't really need a 4, but I needed to avoid a 6. Laying up was the smart play.

JoAnne, on the other hand, had to make something happen. She figured she needed a 4 to tie and went for the green in two. Her shot barely carried the pond. She had a poor lie, making for an awkward stance, and a huge tree stood between her and the green. She had two chances: slim and none.

But Carner is Carner. After I hit a mediocre approach 40 feet from the hole, she played her shot—and what a shot it was! With one foot in the water, she opened the blade of her wedge and gave the ball a great slash. Grass and mud flew everywhere, and the ball shot up over the tree and landed five feet from the hole. The crowd went wild. I couldn't believe she had managed to hit that shot, especially under so much pressure.

All of a sudden, my forty-footer looked like a four-hundred-footer. If she makes her putt for a 4, and I two-putt, we have a playoff. I was tempted to take a real run at my putt, but then I figured that she still has a putt she has to make, and if I stick with my strategy and play for no worse than five, I can still win. What I needed to avoid is being too bold, three-putting, and beating myself. Besides, I'm pretty comfortable in playoffs.

My approach putt stopped 3½ feet from the hole. JoAnne then lipped out her five-footer and I made my putt to win. I had stuck with my game plan and trusted my instincts. I'd also beaten one of the best players in the history of the game—but I had to play one of my greatest rounds to do it.

Trust Your Instincts: the 1983 Nabisco-Dinah Shore

For as long as I can remember, this tournament has been something very special to me. It's not just that it's one of our majors, although that certainly gives it an edge over most events. And it's not because it's played in the Palm Springs area, which is sort of my backyard. It's really a combination of factors, beginning with Dinah herself and ending with the prestige that goes with winning her tournament.

In 1983, the wind was the story of the tournament. Sunday, it came crashing out of the mountains, blowing at speeds up to 45 mph. I've always been a good wind player, but like everyone else I struggled under these conditions. I wound up winning, and there were two shots in the final round that were key.

The first came on the 15th hole at Mission Hills, which is my least favorite hole in golf. It's a fairly short par 4, with an out of bounds down the left side and a grove of trees in the landing area. It's a funny thing, but sometimes a hole just never fits your eye, and as a result, you never seem to play it very well. I figure this hole alone has cost me three or four wins at Mission Hills.

As usual, I hit a poor drive here, dumping it into the trees. I needed to hook a 6-iron for my approach, but if I hooked it too much—or the wind caught it more than I planned—I stood a good chance of hitting the ball out of bounds. I had a one-shot lead, which wasn't enough to let me play safe and lay up. Fortunately, the shot came off exactly as I'd planned, and I managed to get away from the hated 15th with a par and my lead intact.

The 18th is a good par five guarded by water down the left side. Your approach is to an island green. It's one of the best finishing holes we play all year.

Still leading by a shot, I took the water out of play by hitting my drive into the right rough. The hole was playing dead into the wind, and after hacking my 7-wood out of the rough, I was left with 172 yards to carry the water and 190 yards to the pin. Again, the shot would be directly against the wind, with the green surrounded by water.

Both my caddie and this little voice in my head was telling me to lay up short of the water and play for five. Call it ego or guts or just sheer craziness, but I never really doubted for a second that I would go for it. I knew I wouldn't be able to sleep at night if I layed up. I'd rather go down with both barrels blazing, playing aggressively, than to win by playing safe.

I took a 3-iron and hit a pure and perfect draw that held its line in the wind, landing forty feet to the right of the hole. Two putts later I had won my seventeenth tour event. And just as important to me, I had trusted my instincts and won the tournament like a champion.

A master of timing and tempo, Amy is known as a savvy mental player, especially under tough conditions. To get a proper tempo and to keep her mind off the pressure in tournament golf, she uses a "One, Two, Three" drill for her swing—a drill she says she "holds on to like a life preserver." On one, she makes a forward press and begins her backswing. Two, takes her to the top of her swing, and on three, she makes contact with the ball. Amy uses this non-nonsense drill for every swing type from putting to full swings, and she feels it has given her an edge in tournament play.

What My Father Taught Me

Patty Sheehan, with Robert Carney
from "Golf Digest," June 1986

Although her athletic career began on the ski slopes as a champion skier, Patty Sheehan quickly became one the most dominant players on the LPGA Tour. After winning several amateur tournaments, including the Nevada State Championship from 1975 to 1978 and the California Amateur in 1978 and 1979, she joined the tour in 1980. She has captured several major victories including the 1983, 1984, and 1993 LPGA championships, and the 1992 and 1994 United States Women's Open Championship. In 1992, she won the Women's British Open, and in 1996 she won her thirty-fifth tournament and her sixth major championship at the Nabisco-Dinah Shore Winner's Circle. She qualified for the LPGA Hall of Fame in 1993 after her thirtieth win. The following essay is a tribute to her father.

In more ways than I sometimes like to admit, I'm a chip off the old block—my dad, Bobo Sheehan. My father introduced me to golf and, though I competed mostly against my three brothers, I think I've inherited his timing. I've certainly got his strong hands through the ball.

But it's more than that. My dad exposed me to golf in a way that gave me the chance to excel, but never so that I didn't enjoy it. From the time I followed him and Mom around the course at Middlebury, Vermont, when I was four, he never pushed me. But he did encourage me. And he encouraged me to be good.

Some of my fellow LPGA players have said that I'm a tenacious competitor, that I'm tough under pressure. I learned patience from my mother, but I got that toughness from Dad. He is one of the most competitive people I've ever met. He was a great athlete, especially a great skier; and he coached the U.S. Olympic men's Alpine team in 1956. He coached football, baseball, golf, and skiing at Middlebury College. Although I didn't have a chance to see him compete, I know how competitive he was by how he taught me to compete.

One day in particular comes to mind, an incident I remember often on the golf course. I was eleven and had won my first national ski title the previous year. I was racing in a downhill event at Alpine Meadows, and as I came out of the gate, I caught the tip of my ski and spun around. I started to cry because I thought the race was over. But as I did I caught sight of my dad at the side of the run. "Get going!!" he yelled. And I took off as fast as I could because I knew I was in trouble. Despite that horrible start, I finished fourth in the race. And I learned the lesson he most wanted me to learn: Never give up. Some of the caddies call me "Sunday Patty" because I am apt to shoot a very low score on Sunday. They never count me out. Chalk that up to Bobo.

Dad always said, "There's no use competing if you're not going to win," but in skiing, as in golf, the *choice* to compete was always mine.

When I was thirteen I decided to give up competitive skiing because I was burned out. It was a big crisis for me. I knew that Dad had dreamed of one of us becoming an Olympic skier, and I was sure when I told him of my decision he would be disappointed and angry. I agonized over how to tell him. Finally

I called and said, "I don't want to do this anymore." Dad said, "Fine. I've frozen enough of my life. Why should you have to?"

But all sports were great to Dad. At home in Vermont, sports took place around the house. We had a sand pit for the pole vault. We had a ski jump in the backyard. We had a miniature golf course in the backyard—the putting green was in the garage—and our house was just off a real golf course so we could play almost whenever we wanted. Dad never confused us with a lot of mechanics when he coached. In skiing we weren't pretty, but we could get down the hill fast. In golf, he just said, "Keep your eye on the ball." To this day, I don't get bogged down in swing analysis.

That's my dad. As tough as he is, as competitive as he is, he always made sports fun for me. If it looks like I'm having a good time on the golf course, that comes from him. He's a good player himself, at age 63 a 6-handicapper at Hidden Valley Country Club in Reno. And he likes to win. He played (and lost to) my brother Butch for the club championship there. But when Dad hits a bad shot, or if he had a bad day, he just laughs. He has always told us to have fun. As a coach he was, and is, the life of the party. Now, no matter where I go around the country, people come up to me and ask me if Dad is there. Well, he is. Right beside me.

I'm not versed in all the mechanics of the golf swing, but teachers who see my father and me swing say there are some strong similarities. Our tempo and timing are similar. My dad makes a smooth, unhurried swing. We both swing our hands inside the target line early on the backswing and come at the ball from the inside. We both make a good hip turn. Our hand action through the ball, I think, is similar. We both draw the ball.

The differences stem primarily from differences in strength between him and me, and between most men and most women. To compensate for his strength advantage, I developed a stronger grip than my dad's—that is, the right hand is turned farther right.

I get off my left side on the backswing a little better than Dad does for a longer backswing and more clubhead speed. Dad needs a little less leg action because he has a lot more strength in his arms.

But teachers say that if you added just a little upward arm movement to Dad's swing, and subtracted the additional wrist cock I get because of my stronger grip, we'd have a pretty similar swings. Having said all of this, let me give you the bottom line: I can still out drive him!

Patty Sheehan is known for her consistent and precise putting, but she had many near misses and disappointments in the United States Women's Open Championship. The title just seemed to elude her until 1992 at Oakmont Country Club in Pittsburgh. On the final day of the tournament, she was two strokes back before play was delayed because of lightning. Sitting in the clubhouse, Patty told herself not to give up, and when play resumed, she birdie the 17th and drained an 18-foot birdie putt on the 72nd hole to force a play-off with Juli Inkster. She went on to win the tournament, showing the force of sheer determination.

Win Some, Lose Some

Nancy Lopez
from *The Education of a Woman Golfer*, 1979

The darling of American golf, Nancy is one of the most popular and successful athletes of recent times. After she won the New Mexico Women's Amateur at the age of twelve, she was on her way to being the next superstar of women's golf.

She credits her father, Domingo Lopez, for introducing her to the game at the young age of eight and for sacrificing their small income to help her take lessons. As a Mexican-American, Nancy felt the effects of discrimination, but her warm and friendly personality made her a crowd favorite when she joined the tour in 1977. In 1978 fans watched her amazingly win tournament after tournament—capturing nine victories, including a record five wins in a row. In 1979, she won another eight tournaments. She was awarded the Rolex Player of the Year Award four times and the Vare Trophy three times, and in 1987 she captured her thirty-fifth tournament win, earning her the privilege of becoming a LPGA Hall of Fame member. Here she describes how she won five times in a row.

The first thing I do after losing, regardless of whether I lost a close one because of a silly lapse or simply was snowed under by a rival running on a hot streak, is to forget it. I take a look at my calendar and start thinking about where we'll be playing next week, and I'll show 'em then! Remember the lyr-

ics in the song "Many a New Day" from the show *Oklahoma?*
The show was long before my day, but the movie is always being
revived and the girl tells about not ever looking back, but always
looking ahead. She sings that she never asks an August sky what
happened to last July.

That's me, and that's a substantial part of my education in
philosophy. For example, let me tell you about what happened
in the course of my rookie year on the tour in 1978.

If you're interested enough in me at all to be reading this,
you probably know more or less about the beginning. After a
couple of first efforts in tournaments early in the year, in which
I predictably did nothing much, I broke into the winner's circle
for the first time as a pro in the Bent Tree Classic at Sarasota, Florida. I don't know if winning any other tournament will
ever again mean quite as much to me, and not only because it
was my first victory. I had just returned to the tour after my
Mom's death and somehow, knowing how much she loved me
and how much she wanted me to make good, I became stronger
mentally for her sake.

It was a seventy-two-hole tournament and I was well satisfied with my first round 71, but it was only good enough to
place me two strokes back of Hollis Stacy's spectacular 69, one
back of Betsy King's 70, and in a tie for third with Laura Baugh.
Over the next eighteen Hollis, who was going to play so consistently a few weeks later in winning the U.S. Open, blew up to a
78 and shot her way out of this tournament, and Laura did the
same. But Betsy reeled off a neat 71, one stroke less than my 72,
and took the lead by two strokes. Actually JoAnne Carner's 69
was the day's sensation but that, added to her first round of 76,
left her four strokes behind Betsy and two behind me. Donna
White and Amy Alcott were right in there too breathing down
our necks. The third round in a seventy-two-hole affair is often

the one that goes a long way toward settling things, and while Silvia Bertolaccini shot a fine 69 while all of us early leaders were settling for solid but unspectacular rounds in the low 70's, the girl who was really burning up the course was my pal Jo Ann Washam, who posted a 67. So at the end of that third round we were bunched, and Donna White and I in the lead at 216, Jo Ann only one stroke back, Amy Alcott two, and Silvia and Jo-Anne Carner three strokes off the pace. Anybody's tournament.

But Donna soared to a 76 on the final round while I was shooting a 73, good enough to stand up against all the others, and I had won my first professional tournament. My total was 289, one over par for the four rounds, and while I've played better in tournaments both before and since, that first win at Bent Tree meant more to me emotionally than any other.

When I got the lead in the last round I was absolutely determined not to lose it, and I didn't. I remember crying all the way down the seventy-second fairway, knowing that I had the victory pretty well in hand unless I blew it completely, and I couldn't stop crying right through the award ceremony, at which I dedicated my win to my mother's memory. No matter what else lies in store for me in gold, Bent Tree will always be something very special.

Right after that, in the next tournament, the Sunstar Classic at the Rancho Park Golf Club in Los Angeles, I won again, and now people started to sit up and take notice of me. A number of newspaper articles and magazine stories about me began to appear and I have to admit that it was fun. Also, I had now won two big-money purses and the Lopez family was beginning to see more money than they had ever seen before. I was starting to repay my Dad's unbounded love and confidence in me, and it would have been perfect if only my dear Mom had been around to share in it all.

But after Sunstar and the early splash of publicity, Jack Nicklaus's percentage theory caught up with me. I kept playing pretty well, but there are a lot of wonderful women golfers on the tour and no one was hanging around waiting for this rookie to walk all over them. In my next five tournaments the best I could do was to finish second in one, the Kathryn Crosby/Honda Civic Classic, but my next best was no better than a tie for fifth, and in one other I finished far down the list in a tie for eighteenth place. Still, life was more than okay. I was having a very gratifying rookie year, with two tournament triumphs already under my belt and prize-money winnings well in excess of $50,000. I really couldn't expect or hope for much more in the half year to go.

What happened next, therefore, might have sprung right out of *Fantasy Stories* or *True Romances*. *I won the next five tournaments IN A ROW,* a feat unmatched in women's golf history. For the record they were:

> Greater Baltimore Classic, Pine Ridge C.C., Lutherville, Md.
> '78 LPGA Coca Cola Classic, Forsgate C.C., Jamesburg, N.J.
> Golden Lights Championship, Wykagyl C.C., New Rochelle, N.Y.
> LPGA Championship, Jack Nicklaus G.C., Kings Island, Ohio
> Bankers Trust Classic, Locust Hill C.C., Rochester, N.Y.

The big one, of course, was the fourth-in-a-row win, my taking of the LPGA Championship. It was the tournament up to then that carried the greatest prestige and that I wanted dear-ly to win, and everything came up roses for me over those four days. My first round of 71 wasn't anything exceptional but it was good enough to put me right up there, and the next day when I really got hot with a second round of 65, I guess it became sort of discouraging for everybody else. I had a nine-hole stretch in that round, from the ninth hole through the seventeenth, where I shot eagle, birdie, par, par, birdie, eagle, par, birdie, birdie. Dad called it right when he yelled, some place near the end of that run, "Nancy, that ball got eyes!"

I stayed sky high for the final two rounds, shooting a 69 and a 70 for a total seventy-two-hole score of 275 over Jack Nicklaus's 6,312-yard Golf Center Course. That was thirteen strokes under par and left me with a fat six-stroke lead over Amy Alcott, the runner-up. It was just a super tournament for me in every way, being such an important one, having played so well, doing it while my Dad was watching, and keeping my streak of consecutive wins going so that now I'd won four in a row. That tied the record to date shared by Mickey Wright, Kathy Whitworth, and Shirley Englehorn. If I could just win my next tournament, I'd have the record all to myself.

So I headed for the Bankers Trust Classic in Rochester riding high and feeling very determined. But there sure were a lot of distractions throughout the early part of that week. First a golf match for me was arranged where I played with former President Gerald Ford. That was a thrilling experience even if the golf was no better than ordinary.

The next day I went to New York to appear on the *Good Morning America* show on television, and I was bowled over by how many people recognized me right out on the street walking with my manager. Some actually yelled "Good luck!" to me right out of their car windows. Later, when I got back to Rochester and turned on the TV, there I was hitting balls while Carly Simon sang "Nobody Does It Better" as the background. Wow!

We had a day of practice coming up the following morning, and I figured I'd have a chance to settle down a bit before the tournament. But believe it or not, when I showed up at the practice tee, where usually no one is around except the players, several hundred people had turned out just to see me take some swings! I almost had to fight my way through my well-wishers to get to the clubhouse for lunch.

Once the tournament started I played pretty well, but my 72 on the first eighteen could have been a bit better. It was good enough so that I was only one stroke off the pace, but something happened at the beginning of the back nine that really shook me up. My drive went off line from the tenth tee and went into the crowd of spectators lining the fairway some two-hundred yards or more out. And it hit a man named Dr. Jerry Mesolella right on the head. I rushed up there and burst into tears as I saw him lying on the ground with some blood on his forehead. As I reached out to hold his hand he looked up and said to a friend, "At least I'm going to get a chance to meet her!" So he wasn't badly hurt at all, but if he had been I'm sure I would have dropped out, no matter how important the tournament seemed to me. As it was I kept crying all the way along the hole, after Dr. Mesolella said he was okay and waved me on, and I double-bogeyed it, but I pulled myself together then and scored my 72. The next day I had a 73, which didn't make my chances of winning seem too rosy, but in the third and final day of this fifty-four-hole event, I managed to cut loose and banged out a 4-under-par 69. That did it. My total of 214 was good enough to beat Jane Blalock and Debbie Massey by two strokes. At the presentation ceremony I blew a kiss to Dr. Mesolella and thanked him for his encouragement. Everything might have been very different if he'd been a different sort of person, or if he'd happened to have been hurt badly.

So now I had really pulled it off. Five straight tournament wins for a new record, and starting right then I guess I became a real, honest-to-goodness celebrity.

A Matter of Pride

Nancy Lopez
from *The Complete Golfer,* 1987

If there is one characteristic that all great champions share, it's an enormous sense of pride. That's true in all walks of like. The people who excel are those who are driven to show the world—and prove to themselves—just how good they are.

It may seem like a small thing, but did you ever see a great player who looked like a dirt-bag? I've never seen one. All the great players I've seen keep themselves in good shape, are well groomed, and dress nicely. It's a matter of self-image. If you look good, you'll feel good about yourself, and that can't help carrying over into your golf—or any other endeavor.

I know that I can't play well if I don't think I look good. That's one very pragmatic reason that I've made it a point to get my weight back to normal after giving birth to both Ashley and Erinn. My father always used to kid me, saying, "Ten more pounds, ten more yards," but enough was enough!

It also carries over in equipment. I need to have spotless clubs in order to play my best. I sometimes play with people who have so much dirt and grass on their clubs that it's a wonder they ever hit a solid shot. Again, I think it's a matter of pride, and more often than not, most golfers I see with equipment in that condition don't have much pride in their game.

Still, looking nice and having well-kept clubs are just a small part of having pride. True competitors love the challenge of putting their pride on the line and responding. As I look back on my career, I know I've played my best golf when my pride was either hurt or challenged—by either another player or the situation. And that's true for all great players. Look at Sam Snead and Ben Hogan. They brought out the best in each other's game when they went head-to-head. Or how about Jack Nicklaus when another player came along to challenge his domination of the men's tour? Think of the classic rivalries he had over the years with Arnold Palmer, Lee Trevino, Johnny Miller, and Tom Watson. It wasn't anything personal. It's just that when the starter says, "Play away," your pride is on the line and the game is on. I know that, for me, that's when golf is really the most fun.

I can think of plenty of times when I felt I had something to prove and couldn't wait to get out and prove it. JoAnne Carner said she was going to "leave me in the dust" at the Golden Lights tournament in New York. I went on to win, and it was one of the wins in my streak of five straight in 1978. I learned a lot about being a competitor during that streak.

I'm not a believer in false modesty, and when I came out on tour I knew I was good. But until I got on that streak in 1978, I didn't really appreciate just how good a player I was. It was like the rest of the tour just stood still. It's a funny thing about a streak, but it has a snowball effect. I was playing well, so my confidence was high. Because I was so confident, my concentration level was very high, and I didn't let little things distract me. It also meant that I could finesse more shots than I ordinarily would. And last but not least, because I was playing so well, the other players were looking over their shoulders, worrying about what I was going to do next. All the pieces were falling into place. I didn't have room for any negative thoughts. All I knew was that I was playing well and loving every minute of it. Anyone who was going to stop my streak was going to have to deal with one mad little Mexican in the final round. My pride was on the line.

Eventually, of course, my streak did end. Nobody can sustain a concentration level that high for that long. And after five weeks I was physically and mentally tired. But something else happened along the way. I noticed that the other players lifted the level of their game. Their pride was on the line as well, and toward the end of that magical five weeks I could no longer go out and win with par on the last day.

Several years later, at the 1985 LPGA Championship, I got as mad as I've ever been on the golf course, but instead of letting my anger destroy my chances in the tournament I made it work to my advantage, which is something I think all good competitors manage to do.

Playing in the third round, I was paired with Janet Coles and Chris Johnson. Both were struggling through difficult rounds, while I was playing the best round of my career. Usually it's pretty hard to shoot a good score when your playing companions are grinding. Play is slower than you'd like, and it's tough to concentrate, especially when the other players are hitting the ball all over the lot, and you have to wait for rulings.

Sure enough, on our 12th hole the officials came out to tell us we had fallen 27 minutes behind the previous group and that we were going to be timed. That only added to the pressure, because we were very conscious that we had just 45 seconds for each shot, no matter how difficult.

Still, coming into the closing holes, I was on my way to an outstanding score that might put the tournament out of reach. On the 7th hole—which was really our 16th hole—I knocked my approach three inches from the cup for a birdie.

Pumped up, I hit a good 4-iron on the next hole, a par three, and made par. As I walked off the green the officials told me I'd taken 86 seconds on that shot and was going to be penalized.

I couldn't believe it. The greatest round of my life, and I'm being penalized for slow play. First of all it's not even my fault we're out of position, and second of all, there's no living way that shot took almost a minute and a half to play. As hard as I tried not to, I broke down in tears of anger and frustration. Chris and Janet felt terrible, but there wasn't anything they could do.

Standing on the final tee, I could barely see the ball through the tears. Somehow I hit a good drive, hit my approach to six feet, and parred out. Without the penalty strokes I would have shot a 63.

The next day I had tunnel vision. I don't remember anything about anyone else's round. I don't remember the galleries. I don't remember the television cameras or anything else. All I knew was that I was going to show the LPGA and its officials and its rulings that I could win in spite of them all. I promise you, nobody could have beaten me that day. Nothing could have happened that would have cost me that tournament. I got into a zone where I could see every shot before I hit it, and every shot was perfect in my mind.

I got more satisfaction from that win than any other before or since. And I doubt that if I win another 100 tournaments, any of them will ever give me as much pure satisfaction.

The point I want to make is that a competitor will find a way to win. Competitors take bad breaks and use them to drive themselves just that much harder. Quitters take bad breaks and use them as reasons to give up. It's all a matter of pride.

Concentration

People often ask me whether I think Ashley and Erinn will become good golfers. I think it's a little early to tell, but I do know that at age four Ashley concentrates a lot better than most kids her age. If she is looking at a book, the world can fall apart around her and she'll still be looking at that book. When I take her to the golf course, she'll take her little club and focus as hard as she can on whacking the ball. Nobody will ever accuse her of having a swing like Mickey Wright's, but then nobody's saying her mother does either.

The ability to concentrate is a characteristic all good competitors must have. You need to be able to focus fully on each shot, one shot at a time. You can't get too high or too low about the previous shot or hole. And you can't worry about what's going to happen two holes from now. You have to live in the present on the course.

Whenever people talk about competitors with great concentration, Ben Hogan's name comes up. According to one story, he was paired with Claude Harmon in the Masters one year when Harmon aced the par-three 12th. The large gallery went wild; the roar was enormous.

As they walked to the next tee, Hogan turned to Harmon and asked, "Claude, what did you make there?"

"Why Ben, I made a one," said a startled Harmon.

"Oh," said Hogan and wrote the figure on his scorecard.

Now that's concentrating! I don't think many people can concentrate that well. I'm not even sure they should try. But for the minute or so that it takes to plan a shot, address the ball, and hit it, I think your game deserves your undivided attention.

As I mentioned in my last essay, my concentration was severely tested in Rochester in 1978. I was going for my fifth straight win, and things weren't going very well in the final round. I had been hooking the ball badly off the tee for the entire front nine and was struggling.

As I stood on the 10th tee, the large gallery stretched down both sides of the hole. Instead of hooking the ball, I hit it straight right, hitting a spectator on the head and knocking him to the ground. There was blood all over the place.

"Oh, my gosh," I said, as my heart pounded and I raced to see how badly he was hurt.

"Oh please stay in bounds," said my caddie, Roscoe, who apparently didn't have any problems with his concentration.

The spectator, Dr. Gerry Mesollela, said he was fine and urged me to get back out and play. I was so shaken, I wasn't sure I'd ever be able to hit another ball, much less play again.

I double-bogeyed the hole and didn't see any way I could regroup. Winning the tournament was the furthest thing from my mind. All I could see was the blood.

As I walked to the next tee, I made a deal with myself. I decided to dedicate the tournament to Gerry. Once I did that, I was able to put the accident out of my mind and concentrate on the job at hand. Sure enough, I won, and Gerry has been a good friend ever since.

Competition and Friendship

Everybody likes to win or so they say. The truth of the matter is that some people shy away from really turning on the heat because they're afraid they might lose friends if they keep beating them. I can't say I've ever worried much about that, but I know it happens.

Successful competitors want to win. Head cases want to win at all costs. Those are the people who would cheat, cut corners, or run over their grandmothers just to get their name on a silver cup. Competitors just want to go out there, do their best, and shake hands when it's all over.

It all comes down to a question of priorities. When I'm on the course, it's my job to concentrate fully, do my best, and try to win. If the person I happen to beat is a friend, I have to hope he or she realizes that it's nothing personal. We're both out there for the same reason. If you lose a friend because you've won fair and square, that person probably wasn't much of a friend to begin with.

JoAnn Washam is one of my best friends on tour. Early in my career we'd occasionally room together to save on expenses.

On one occasion, we came into the final round at Costa Mesa paired in the last group. Things weren't what you'd call tense in the room Saturday night, but the atmosphere wasn't as relaxed as it normally would be. Both of us knew that, if we were going to win, we had to beat the other player. If we went out and played like friends, someone else would come along and beat us both. I wanted to win. If I didn't, I wanted JoAnn to win. I sure didn't want someone else to come along and win because we were too worried about each other.

JoAnn and I talked about it and decided that we'd try to act like we weren't friends when we got to the course. That worked until we walked off the first tee: then I couldn't stand it any longer.

"JoAnn, this is just killing me," I said. "I have to know what you're thinking.

That was fine for a while, but things did tighten up on the final nine. She had me by two shots with four holes to play. I went birdie-birdie and finally won.

I went back to the room with mixed feelings. I was glad I had won, but I felt badly that I had to beat JoAnn to do it.

The hard truth is that, no matter how much you might like someone, once you tee it up, your friends become acquaintances until the last putt is holed. That may sound cold, but that's the toughest part of being a competitor.

And that's where your soul-searching has to begin.

In the late 70s, Nancy Lopez helped to reintroduce the game of golf to an entire generation of women. Soon every little girl wanted to be just like Nancy. Although her greatest attribute is her ability to maintain exactly the same tempo each time she plays, she considers her mind her greatest strength in golf, and she teaches that if you are playing poorly, you should stop and look at how beautiful the course is, substituting a positive thought for a negative one and changing your whole attitude in a moment.

A Good Man Is Hard to Find—
Golf and the Opposite Sex

Helen Alfredsson
from *A Good Swing is Hard to Find*, 1998

Seven time Swedish National champion, Helen Alfredsson was one of the most aggressive and daring players on tour. By the time she was thirteen years old, she had a nine handicap, and soon after that she was dividing her time between playing for the Swedish National Golf Team and working as a model in Paris. She moved to San Diego to attend the International University and then in 1990 won the Weetabix Women's British Open. In 1992 she became the LPGA Rookie of the Year, and she clenched her first LPGA major by winning the 1993 Nabisco-Dinah Shore Winner's Circle. She took home three LPGA wins from 1994-1998; the Ping/Welch's championship, the Office Depot, and Welch's Circle K Championship. She has been a five-time member of the Solheim Cup team.

Here, she gives advice that should prove helpful to many women; how to approach playing golf with men.

At the Women's Open in Southern Pines, North Carolina, two years ago I had dinner with some guests of a corporate golf sponsor. One of them was remarking how she had played a round of golf earlier in the day with another woman who consistently hit her drives farther than she did. This upset the woman I was having dinner with because, as she explained, she was almost always longer off the tee than anyone else and so she couldn't figure out who this other woman was. A second dinner guest, who knew the mystery woman golfer in question, quickly explained that "she" was a "he" the year before!

Let's face it, men and women, even if they change their sexual identity, will always feel competitive with one another. When women tell me that it is sometimes frustrating to play golf with men, I tell them, "That's why we have handicaps." Handicaps will always level the playing field with a group of golfers of varying skills. But I know it doesn't do much to alleviate the intimidation factor. I always think the best way of breaking the ice is by using sarcasm, and saying something like "Aren't you lucky today, you get to play with a woman. Maybe you'll learn something."

Sometimes I've broken the ice inadvertently. I once played golf with the actor Sidney Poitier, who was very polite but somewhat reticent. I was sharing a cart (the club required them) with a female friend, and we decided to remove the windshield so we could get some sun. With no place to put the windshield, we simply laid it at our feet. At some point in the round, while we were all mulling over our shots in the fairway, the cart suddenly took off on its own. The windshield had fallen against the gas pedal and the cart went careening down a hill out of control, with me in fast—but not fast enough—pursuit. Luckily the cart crashed into some bushes. It was a good thing, because I was laughing so hysterically I would have never caught up with it. I'm not sure what Sidney Poitier thought of me that day, but I know he had at least one good laugh.

It's amazing, though, how often men are the ones running away when they see a woman approaching their threesome on the first tee. The assumption is always that the woman golfer will slow them down. I know very fine women amateurs who still hear comments from men like "You play pretty good for a girl." Even when that "girl" is in her forties and has a 16-handicap.

The most important thing to remember is to play your own game. As women we have to get over the inhibition factor. More than likely, the men we play with are just as self-conscious as we are. They are usually so often caught up in the macho thing and not even paying attention to how you're playing. Then again, sometimes they just embarrass themselves.

A few years ago I was playing in a pro-am in Japan where I was paired with the president of the Nichirei Corporation, which was sponsoring the LPGA tournament I was to play in that week. After stepping up to the first tee, he took a few practice swings, paused over the ball, then brought his club back and took a mighty ... whiff. He actually fell on his butt! To his credit, he was a good sport about it—he kind of had to be—and laughed heartily. So did I.

It can be difficult, though, when you're paired with men who get really uptight when you're outplaying them. What I like to do, again, is be sarcastic in order to loosen things up. If I miss a putt, I might say, "Oops, my skirt blew up." If we can use our own stereotypes to joke about ourselves, we can make playing with men so much more comfortable. When we make fun of ourselves in this way we're also telling those guys who still say things like "Nice putt, Alice" when they miss a short one, that we know how they think. Women never talk disparagingly of men when they miss a putt. So when I'm playing with a male amateur, I'll kid with him when he misses a putt and say something like "Oh, did you drop your lipstick on that one?" Hopefully it sounds so ridiculous to him that we can both laugh at the joke. The bottom line is, playing golf isn't any fun if you're not having any fun playing.

Helen shot a 63 in the first round of the 1994 United States Women's Open Championship. However, during the middle of Saturday's round, her game suddenly disintegrated and she began to lose her lead. She began to think she needed things to happen: she needed to play perfectly, she needed to hit fairways and to make putts. In the end, she lost the match to Patty Sheehan. Although the experience was painful for her, Helen believes she learned a valuable lesson; that you should never need to make every shot, but rather you should always stay positive and believe in yourself no matter how you are playing.

Afterword

The idea for this book came to me one afternoon, after a particularly great game of golf. I was so thrilled to have played well that I wanted to read what other great women golfers had to say about this exciting game. After considerable searching, I found a 1933 essay entitled "Two Matches with Glenna" by golfing great Joyce Wethered. I was captivated by her elegant writing and her charming way of describing the famous 1929 Ladies' British Open Amateur Championship match between her and Glenna Collett. I also found myself engrossed to find out who won—rooting for Joyce at first, but then later rooting for Glenna when I discovered that this was the one title she never captured during her golfing career.

That essay led me to search for others by women golfers, and I found that many of the great women players did take the time to recount their personal anecdotes on golf. I thought that these insightful and significant tales were told richly and complexly, but more important, they gave a woman's point of view on golf.

Women approach golf in ways we can all relate to. When Rhona Adair, for example, tells us that women seem to know how to play better under pressure situations, observing that we possess some "inner strength and pluck," I recognize that determination when I watch the great women players of today. I only wish they took the time to write about their golf game as these pioneers once did. Alas, we do have social media to help us gain some insight to their games.

But there isn't a golfer who can't relate to Jane Blalock's butterflies and clammy hands when she's about to make an important putt, or Joyce Wethered when she writes of her "knees were inclined to be unsteady; the tee seemed vast and empty space" as she teed off from the first hole. I feel something like that every time I tee it up. The only difference is that in Joyce's case, she had hundreds of people watching her from the clubhouse and sidelines.

When I have an off day in golf, I take great comfort in reading about Glenna Collett's embarrassing first tournament round. She was ready to give up the game, thinking that she would never be good at it. Many of the women in this book—Kathy Whitworth, Betsy Rawls, and Mickey Wright—had similar experiences, where things were not going their way. They vowed to quit golf forever, but the thrill of hitting the ball far down the fairway and their love of the game made them more determined. There was an inner sense that they had it within them to master the game and win tournaments. They went to the practice range, hitting balls until their hands were blistered or until dusk when the range shut down. Driven, they struggled to be their best. They often talked to themselves, saying words of encouragement or stinging words of motivation. They knew they hadn't worked so hard to give up a championship over a single clutch putt or a playoff hole. Their willpower was so strong that the ball simply had to obey.

When they did come back, it was usually with tremendous results. Glenna Collett, for example, went on to win the United States Women's Amateur Championship six times, and Kathy Whitworth, with eighty-eight professional victories, holds the record for tour wins, male or female. Mickey Wright's third win at the United States Women's Open Championship gave her "the secret satisfaction of a little girl with a most cherished possession." I have a picture of her with her arms wrapped tight around the trophy and the look of great pride.

Winning, however, meant fulfilling their dreams and many of the pioneer women golfers were raised to believe that competing in any sport, let alone a golf match, was improper. Despite public judgement for their "unladylike" manners, the lure of golf called to them and they tirelessly worked for acceptance.

Through their writings, they have recorded for us their personal historical perspective on the game—from the days where they had to wear long full skirts to play and were always limited to the time they could play, to the early LPGA days where Babe, Patty, and Betsy joined together with others to form an organization that gave women golfers the recognition they deserved.

No matter if you are just taking up the game or have played your whole lifetime, I hope you have enjoyed your visit with them in the women's clubhouse—visit them again sometime.

Terri Leonard

December 2016

Credits

Grateful acknowledgment is made for permission to include the following previously copyrighted material in this edition:

From *Gettin' to the Dance Floor*, "You're Always Learning New Ideas, New Methods," and "You Don't Have the Responsibilities People Have in the Real World," by Al Barkow. Copyright © Burford Books and Classics of Golf publishers. Used by permission of the publishers.

From *Golf for Women*, "It's All in Your Head," by Louise Suggs. Copyright © 1960 by Rutledge Books. Used by permission.

From *Play Golf the Wright Way*, "This One's on Me," by Mickey Wright, edited by Joan Flynn. Copyright © 1962 by Mickey Wright and Joan Flynn. Used by permission of the author.

From *Golf for Women* "Beginnings on the Road with the LPGA," by Kathy Whitworth, with Rhonda Glenn. Copyright © 1990 by St. Martin's Press/ McMillian publishers. Used by permission of McMillian Publishers.

From *A Natural Way to Golf Power*, "My Game of Golf," by Judy Rankin and Michael Aronstein. Excerpt from pp. 3-15. Copyright © 1976 by Judy Rankin and Michael Aronstein. Reprinted by permission of HarperCollins Publishers.

From *The Golfing Mind, My Personal Revelation*," by Vivien Saunders. Copyright © 1984 by Vivien Saunders. Reprinted with the permission of Scribner, a Division of Simon & Schuster, Inc. All rights reserved.

From *The Guts to Win*, "Pressure Golf," by Jane Blalock. Copyright © 1977 by *Golf Digest*. Used by permission of the author.

From *Amy Alcott's Guide to Women's Golf*, "Taking on Tournament Challenges," by Amy Alcott with Don Wade. Copyright © 1991 by Dutton Publishers. Used by permission of the author.

From *Golf Digest* magazine, "The Main Things My Father Taught Me" by Patty Sheehan, with Robert Carney. Copyright © June 1986, The New York Times Company Magazine Group, Inc. All rights reserved. Used by permission of Golf Digest magazine and the author.

About the Author

TERRI LEONARD is an avid, amateur golfer who is a member of EWGA and the Stonetree Golf Club in Novato, California. She has been published in *Golf for Women* magazine and GottaGoGolf online magazine and is the executive managing editor for HarperOne Publishers, an imprint of HarperCollins Publishers, where they hope to publish Nancy Lopez's biography. *In the Women's Clubhouse* was first published by Contemporary Books in 2000 during the LPGA's 50th anniversary. Please send any inquiries to inthewomensclubhouse@aol.com.

*All proceeds from the sale of
this book will go to Girls Golf.
Visit them at GirlsGolf.org.*

Made in the USA
Las Vegas, NV
18 April 2023

70756159R00166